mADD man

A Memoir

By, Brian J. Robinson

ISBN 978-0-557-34122-1

Dedicated to my friends and family, especially my parents who have never stopped believing in me and loving me.

To, Rochelle Castellano, for being a constant source of wisdom and guidance to me since a young age, and for always having a new book for me to read.

To Max, one of the greatest friends anyone could ever have. I'm so glad everything is back to normal.

To my Grandpa Norman for showing me how to enjoy some of the simpler things in life and for being such a supportive and upstanding individual and role model.

To Scott Hoffman, my old literary agent for believing in this project when it was merely a seedling.

I'd also like to thank the following people for being great, and for having an important impact on my life in one way or another throughout the good times and the not so good times:

Allie Shapero, Justin Schanzer, Jesse Richmand, Morgan Dub, Ahmad Mohtadi, Aunt Julie Shuman, Dan and Daniel Schwartz, Eliza Weiss, Brian Lee, Jeanette McNertney, Patrick LoBrutto and all the ATO's.

And a very special thanks to you, the reader, for supporting this project, without which, I'd be at ground zero.

Note: Skip the prologue if you are not into philosophy

Prologue: An Exercise in Maddness

It is almost 2007 and I am ready to die.

So I'll begin my story with a cliché. Perhaps I already have...

It is not that I want to die--I am in fact happy -- it is that I do not fear death. Something tells me I have been here before, or maybe I am comfortable with the idea that not knowing or understanding does not necessarily equate to something bad, evil, or wrong.

As I see it, the fear of death epitomizes what the human intellect truly cannot grasp. The realm of death, on the other hand, of non-existence is beyond the full scope of human intellect. We are terribly afraid of what we do not know or understand. We are afraid of strangers and afraid of those who think differently. This is not a novel thought, but we fail to see the universal ramifications of our response to that which we cannot ever know. With most things in this world, we are, only through reason, able to remove fear from the mental equation that allows reason to determine our actions.

We must keep in mind that expectations represent nothing more than possibility, and while possibility, and the probability of possibility has led human beings to wonderful advancements, it has also led us into unimaginable destruction and missed opportunities. We wage war for ideas and ideals we do not fully understand, or based on false information. One of the most enlightened and influential sentiments of western civilization is the idea that we cannot not know anything with absolute certainty. This is all we know for certain. We must learn as a civilization to incorporate the gray area of all things into our mode of thinking. I live in that gray area—or it would seem so to you. This includes people who are different, people who think differently. If we can learn to consider habitual expectations as only one part of the overall analysis of a given situation, we can dissolve fear into reason and attain a higher level of understanding of the world we live in.

It is with great pleasure that I share with you what I have seen in the short time I have lived. I want you to see it as I do. I appreciate each individual who is taking the time to perhaps gain a better understanding of the unique perception of the world that is my own. In the process I hope you will learn more about yourselves. I speak with confidence and with the unquestionable determination of my soul. And it is indeed, a knowing and old soul.

Please do not see me as pretentious, I simply lack the capacity to speak my mind accurately, and I am tired of the shackles of the spoken word. My experiences and knowledge are wholly visual. I long for the proper conversion factor for that which manifests itself as vision but must be communicated through language. It amazes me how the rarest and most sacred things in this world cannot be duplicated with exact precision. I will do my best to process and translate what I know and simultaneously what I do not know, and along the way, we will search for the gray area where truth resides, and where properly sequenced carbon atoms are recognized as diamonds.

This is the story of the 23 years I have lived with myself in a world that was designed for someone else.

Chapter 1: The Dead End, Toms River New Jersey

It occurred to me today with a spontaneous lightning bolt of neuro-stimulative ambition that it is time to write my book. I know what you are thinking. I have absolutely no business writing a book, especially a book auto-biographical in nature. Autobiographies are reserved for sports heroes, influential historical figures, and celebrities. I fit none of the above categories...yet.

I am a suburban-bred Jewish 23 year old young man from an upper middle-class family who found his way into the world of finance. Quite typical you might say. White collar bred and white collar destined. And sure, I would even agree with you, except for one thing: Absolutely nothing about the 23 years I have lived inside this head of mine has been the least bit ordinary. I have come to realize that the experiences I have lived through and my unique perspective on the world are representative of much more than what a childhood ADHD diagnosis could ever explain.

I always knew that I had the tendency to see things quite differently from the way (as I call them) "the Neurotypicals" see things. My earliest memory exists as a lucid visual of my Father smiling with love in his eyes as he picked me up out of my crib. I was crying my eyes out and must have been 2 at the time. Looking back I knew, even then, that if there was one person I would be able to count on in this world, one person who would love and stand by me no matter what, it would be my father. If not for the careful consideration and undying faith that both he, and to an equal degree my mother have shown me throughout the years, especially when I was a young child, the outcome of my life after 23 years could very well be drastically different.

We lived in Toms River, NJ (home of the 1998 Little League World Series Champions) from 1985 to 1990. Apparently my crying pleas for freedom from the barred cage that was my crib transformed into violent statements of protest where I would virtually shake the entire structure until it fell over. Later on I would just climb out, as it seemed a bit more sensible.

If nothing else, Toms River taught me to be physically tough at an early age. The kids in and around Foothill Court were rough. Besides Timmy Williamson, I was the youngest on the cul de sac, rough housing and playing kickball until the sun came down.

Brian Williamson was my best friend at the time and his kid brother, Timmy would march behind us wherever Brian and I went.

It is truly amazing to me how the universe really is tied together by the most delicate and transparent of forces, like ever shifting layers of indistinguishable energy. Most people do not think twice about the power and magnitude of energy that encompasses our existence. Surely our introduction to these matters is "taught" in school, or so I am told. Looking back I realize I never heard a word that was said to me there. From kindergarten through college, most of what was addressed to me in the form of spoken language was as foreign as the Mandarin I would encounter years later in Shanghai. This same effect probably accounts for the utter lack of coherent sound in the vast majority of every memory that resonates in my consciousness. It is like watching a big screen plasma TV with the most technologically progressive picture clarity money can buy. The TV sits behind a thick and perfectly invisible glass wall that manages to magnify your perception of the big picture to even further degrees of intensity, all the while reducing the sound quality to mere vibrations. Luckily, when I am in tune, these vibrations of sound are able to synthesize themselves into visual images. Sound must be converted to pictures in order for me to process, in my own way, what someone is saying. It is like having a screen in my mind's eye.

Welcome to my custom IMAX theatre, where the shiny buttered popcorn and junior mints are plentiful and Albert Einstein and the rest of the spatially inclined autistics enjoy VIP seating and always share a good laugh. Of course we get a younger following as well, especially around report card time where a D average in school is rewarded with a free coke and a daytime matinee on the house. It is the least that can be done after a full marking period of trying to fit ourselves into an educational system designed for the masses, or in mathematical terms, the distribution of individuals closest to the mean. Is it really a wonder why mathematical and scientific leadership is deteriorating in this country? Some of the most brilliant scientific thinkers, the visual thinkers whose thought processes are innately universal and capable of a different type of creative abstraction, the type of thinking that is absolutely necessary for scientific innovation, are falling through the cracks of the educational system, having never been given a shot to explore their expansive minds. Albert Einstein, who is also known to think in pictures, was at one point a high school dropout who struggled enormously with his education.

Einstein thought, when stuck in a dead end job later in his life, that maybe he should work some physics problems in his spare time. Some of the imaginative thinkers of our time are the visual thinkers and often times as I suspect from my own intimate personal experience with the issue, certain types of brilliance are often muted by learning disabilities. I am sure Einstein would agree that learning ability or disability is relative to the educational environment, as it seems all things are relative in theory. If am thinking conceptually, in pictures, and my teacher is subjecting me to tedious rote memorization in words, then I might as well be sitting in a class room pondering my own thoughts and marching to the beat of my own drum in Shanghai, China. There must be something to be said that a culture, whose written language is pictographic, is leaving the United States in the dust as the global scientific leaders and innovators of modern civilization. Riddle me that.

The fact is our country is lagging further and further behind in the highly competitive landscape of scientific innovation and technological progression. With the decline of manufacturing and our dismal status as scientific pioneers on a global scale, clearly something has to change. It is demoralizing that we are in such poor shape intellectually, despite the obvious fact that we still remain a wealthy economic superpower. Complacency and a lack of intellectual and scientific progress can deliver a severe blow to any country fighting to maintain economic supremacy.

The right educational system and the active pursuit of knowledge and innovation is the DNA of a truly great society. We cannot afford to let some of the brightest minds in our country struggle through life as unrealized potential simply because we are so enslaved by our repetitive methods of thought and policy and methodology. Individuals, who could, with the proper teaching style and encouragement, contribute a great deal to society, end up living their whole life believing they are failures, or worse. It is the most brilliant and unique minds that also tend to be the most fragile. Given rigid societal standards and the cookie cutter idea of intelligence and high performance, it is no wonder that some of our greatest gifts walk the streets and are a fertile untapped natural resource.

The public educational system must will itself toward innovation if we are to compete with the intellectual powerhouses of the East. Just as preventative medicine aims to address and deal with a health problem before it is actually a problem, so too must we transform in a time of relative stability before this problem becomes much more urgent. It is painful to watch as the political process is constantly reacting to dilemmas and crises only when situations become near desperate. Chaotic times are the breeding grounds for rushed and poorly thought out decisions. I have a vision that one day in the near future we will wake up and realize that it is too late to act effectively. Potential continued economic supremacy in a global economy is inextricably linked to a long term commitment to maximizing the intellectual capital of this country. Change must be implemented before our road to opportunity becomes a dead end.

Ok, now I'll get off my soapbox and tell you a story.

Chapter 2: Allow me to introduce myself

After the miniature sermon in the last chapter, the inquisitive reader might ask: where do I get the audacity to recommend change of such magnitude without some sort of graduate degree in educational psychology?

I have lived with my mind for 23 years and I am just beginning to believe in my own abilities. Just so you have an idea, my world exists as a lucid display of inter-connected concepts that make up the whole. These concepts are abstractions; from a thing I see ideas and visually they manifest as derivative lines of thought. I get lost in a hypnotic stream of images. I'll look at dirt and think country, from country I see space, from space, notions of identity and culture, from culture I see change, or "time". Suddenly I am pondering distance. All the while as my tangent carries on, I often won't see what's around me externally, or I'll see both. It's like I am living in two worlds at once, and I need to manage them in order to stay functional, but they can never ever intersect. It's actually quite entertaining… Even when I am seemingly there, I am far away. I can literally have a telephone conversation with someone and go through the motions of human interaction while simultaneously I am carried off into a seemingly altogether different universe. There is no real way to control my thoughts. They are like wind blowing, taking on different forms with a disregard for stillness. Amusingly, I've walked into more trees than I'd like to admit while thinking (or, more accurately, dreaming awake), and then I just shrug it off with a smile and keep on trucking.

So they say I have a "learning disorder." I do not process auditory input properly. Sometimes, all I hear is sound with no meaning when somebody talks to me. If I am not visualizing what is being said while simultaneously conceptualizing as part of a global or big picture analysis, I am not thinking at all. Or more succinctly put, I am rocketing into what one of my best friends in high school cleverly described as "Bri Bri Land". Now do not get me wrong, once I dock into the ether I am in a world that is indistinguishably my own. Bri Bri land as I see it, is where the magic of abstraction and intuitive universal knowledge combine with enough energy for one hell of a quantum leap into the great depths of my semi-unconscious mind. This is more than ADHD or a disorder of some kind folks, this is a gift. And it is only recently amidst the worst transformational struggle I have ever been though, that I finally

realized the truth about this state of mind:

I wasn't hearing what people were saying.

I didn't know anything was abnormal about that, or even

that I wasn't processing. I just wasn't self-aware enough that

anything was different between me and others until I was 23 years

old. It is only now that I realize that when someone is talking to me,

without some sort of external intervention or an immense effort

toward concentration (that often fails) I'll be elsewhere in a matter

of seconds.

Let's back up though, because this state of mind has been

the source of so much joy, so much misery, and so much endless

amusement to others that I must do the best I can to tell this story

from the bottom up. My full name, as you probably know by now is

Brian Jeffrey Robinson. My father is Dr. Neil Robinson and my

mother is the lovely Ellen Robinson-- Mrs. Robinson as so many

have happily pointed out...

Second grade was the golden age of my academic

achievement. I was in a snobby private school where I had to put on an itchy suit and tie every day and I used to dominate the tire swing. I took pride in giving my classmates the ride of their life on that swing, a ride that took them out of the real world for a while and into my own playful universe. My favorite move was the tornado; I would dedicate a good 10 seconds to building a strong rotational momentum and right before the release I would nudge the chain I had been holding onto against the very momentum that I worked so hard to create. The result was an entire swing revolving in one direction, while rotating the exact opposite direction. I used to like to think that my tire swing extravaganza was the closest I could get to creating the sensation of being inside the vacuum of a tornado. I figure any ride that can completely disorient your sense of direction is worth the price of admission. I never did get to ride the tornado myself. A couple of my school yard chums used to try to duplicate it for me but it never came close. Somehow, that was ok, though. My mind was its own tornado.

It was always a mystery to me that second grade was the only time I managed to get straight A's. I used to outperform the kids who eventually ended up going to Ivy League schools on almost every test. Looking back I remember the day where I approached Mrs. Lebbaron's desk and she had a note which said, "Brian's Eyes" I asked her if she meant myself, or Brian Bernstein. She told me the note was in reference to me but it was not a big deal, it is just that she noticed I would hand in writing assignments on notebook paper with a clear disregard for the margins. My handwriting was atrocious and I was literally writing all over the paper as if I was painting. To this day I cannot write in between the lines of school notebook paper, spreadsheets, charts, and so forth. It is as if the lines or boxes in front of me do not exist. Thank goodness for word processing because half the time I cannot read my own writing. Early on at Morgan Stanley, my boss would ask me to quote a number for him and I would quote in the hundred-thousands instead of millions and vice-versa.

After second grade, third grade was proving to be a piece of cake as well. I loved my friends but I was extremely unchallenged academically. 3rd grade was monumental for us in our eyes because it was the first time we ever had our own lockers. Jessica Welt and I would play a game where I would happily volunteer to tuck myself in her locker. She would close the door and we both thought it was the greatest thing. It was pitch dark and I could barely move a muscle and I wouldn't have preferred to be anywhere else. Looking back, I think I enjoyed it so much because it gave me the same sensation I used to feel with all the forts I used to build as a child. I would spend hours building the most elaborate blanket forts. My forts were air tight with little green army figures sometimes placed strategically outside to create an even grander façade of fortification. This makes sense to me. While I have long outgrown my blanket fort days, the shield that I have developed, which separates my truest being from the outside world provides me the same protection as my little army figures did. Not much has changed as my shield is virtually impenetrable and remains air tight. The only difference is that the darkness I have become so accustomed is beginning to dissipate and I am ever so slowly beginning to see a vibrant array of color. And this I embrace with open arms because it is much better to be alone in a world of color than darkness, if given the choice.

Interestingly, the girl who used to shut me into darkness and giggle endlessly, proved to be the very young women who would send me on my path toward liberation over a decade later.

The most precious things in life will sometimes show where you least expect them. I have spent so many years in such extreme isolation, that it took me over 23 years to see the one solution I never even bothered to pay credence to: Liberate yourself, or at least try.

Back on point:

Fifth grade started what I see as the beginning of the end. Years and years of underachievement slowly chiseled away at the foundation of what was once thought to be excellence. As a child I was often uncooperative to say the least. Mischief and exploration were ubiquitously magnetic forces no matter where I found my somewhat chaotic self. Destruction was the name of my game as a child, and still managed to manifest itself in other forms as I got older.

One day while tracing the creek behind my house through the untouched backwoods of the small suburban town where I grew up, my best friend Max and I stumbled upon an actual boat stuck in the mud. The creek was by no means a river with only inches to work with at times. Was there a time where the creek ran deep and powerful like a river, only to be downgraded by nature to a creek years later?

5th grade was a tough year for me and things did not get easier for a while. I began to realize soon that I was trapped, just like that boat and even with the best parents one could ever have, and the most expensive psychiatric advisory board an ophthalmologist's salary could buy, no one could possibly understand the sheer complexity of the thoughts streaming through my mind. I was alone, something I realized at a very early age, and it was always going to be that way, and despite the deafening intensity and universal awareness of my being, I was human in every sense of the word. Survival is one our most base and animalistic imperatives and the will to live and live in my own way is not something I ever seriously questioned. Despite my troubles my spirit is unbreakable and my soul too wise and experienced to ever march to a different drum beat from my own. This beat has sure been put to the test, however.

Chapter 3: Hebrew School= Chinese Water Torture

In my usual non-linear display of sequence, let's rewind to what remains a hotbed of conflict inside me to this day. It's time to talk about Hebrew school, though a small tangential detour into Bri Bri land wouldn't hurt to start off the ceremonies; a thought experiment, if you will..

Here's the thing about time. I just don't get it!

I cannot come to terms with sequence because I cannot come to terms with the man made nature of time. Time is a man made invention and my mind has trouble with artificial concepts. Time is simply the human intellect's attempt to quantify "Change". Change is the only constant in the universe and measuring time, as us humans love to do, is our way of creating expectations of change. I would say we gave it a great shot. Whereas most people view life as a series of moments, my intuitive grasp is that there is only one moment, the same moment. The sun will rise and set and we can certainly call it a new day for the sake of creating a schedule for ourselves, the economy, etc. But from a truly intellectual standpoint, don't you think time is more of a gray area than we pay credence to?

Along these lines, is the existence of a tree altered in any way when we choose to divide its square footage into fractionated chunks? Are we not simply applying a tool or a measuring stick in order to calculate based upon our own way of categorizing things? The same could be asked in application to the whole of existence, with a whole by definition existing as one, are we not merely applying a measuring stick in order for us to better grasp the concept of change without actually touching upon something that is real? ...Who knows? I'm probably just procrastinating. Here it goes:

Hebrew school to me was the most insufferable experience of my life. Like Chinese water torture, it just never ended. First Sunday school and then Hebrew school twice a week. Just like in regular school, I never heard a word a teacher was telling me, but that does not for a second mean that I didn't know exactly where they were coming from.

The people who ran the system had the audacity to try to inflict their belief system onto ME. My moral compass was already fairly highly developed and I was exploring new realms by the second, meanwhile I was expected to show up and listen to what the holy one commanded us to do without any justification for his reasoning. While I am not opposed to the idea of faith, imposing it against someone's will has a name: tyranny.

I still cannot bear to step into the wretched hell hole that is Temple Shalom. For years the Hebrew school classroom brought out the worst in me. The first hour consisted of general religious study (I think.) I truly do not believe I heard or learned anything. I cannot recall how many times I was yelled at, had teachers call my house, or was suspended.

I do remember the one day that more or less epitomizes the anger and rage I had for this institution. Mrs. B., whatever her name was had just finished telling us the story of when Abraham, in accordance with G-d's wishes, carried his own son to the top of a mountain with every intent to slay him. G-d asked him to do this as a display of his undying loyalty to him. Immediately, I raised my hand and with more rage than I could even attempt to cover up, (not that I'd want to) I spoke my mind and my heart. I told her with all due respect, if G-d, or anyone else for that matter, instructed me to take my own son up a mountain and slay him, I would tell him to go to hell. As I said, I cannot even recall which number suspension that resulted in. Apparently, only now do they address this very issue with children during Yom Kippur. Wouldn't be the first time my thinking proved to be a little too progressive.

The second hour was just as unbearable as the first. No, it was worse because it required active participation in learning one of the most audibly displeasing languages I had ever heard. I sat there for an hour listening to a language that was so irritating I could feel myself jittering with disgust. I am very sensitive to sound and I felt like I was surrounded by a caucus of rapid fire spitballs! Sorry to offend… But anyway, the right type of music can influence my emotions profoundly while the sudden squawk of a seagull can send me into emotional disarray. The Hebrew language was worse than any sudden animal sound, far worse. I did my best to tune out, but inevitably I would get called on. Of course I was not on the right page and even after the class informed me of the page number I couldn't read Hebrew anyway. The teacher and I would go through the same ritual every class and waste each other's time in the process. I had decided the moment I arrived at Temple Shalom that

I would not learn anything they taught me. This is in stark contrast to normal school where I tried hard but was beginning to think by sophomore year in high school that I was just plain dumb.

Imagine how disheartening it would be if you could not respond intelligently when people spoke to you. Most of the time, though I only realize this now, I was just guessing which words had come out of another's mouth while doing my best to piece together a response based on context and body language. Every once in a while though, the barrier would drop, and I could process spoken language and beautifully bounce answers back at people with charisma.

The lowering of the barrier was normally coupled with some sort of movement on my part. When I am walking, my ability to focus is drastically improved. I never really understood why I would get these temporary highs where I would feel stimulated, and outwardly confident, but in retrospect, I see that there was always kinetics involved. But there was no telling when the next wave of outward charm and intelligence would come. They certainly did not come around too often at Temple Shalom, where requiring students to sit still seemed to be etched on stone tablets.

By twelve years old they had enough of me. The happiest news I heard in a long time came when they told my parents they don't want me back. I hadn't wanted them for years and I was never given the option of telling them to take a hike.

Looking back, though, it wasn't a total loss. There were two individuals that I did take a liking to. Rabbi Weiner struck me as a man of great character. I do not know whose decision it was after 3 months vacation to invite me back but at the very least I imagine Rabbi Weiner did not object. Imagine my surprise when in one last desperate attempt to get me to become a Bar Mitzvah, I was introduced to a wonderful woman who proved to be a very important person in my life. I knew instantly that she was different. On the rare occasions when I met an authority figure that I actually trusted, I was and still am more than respectful to them. My ability to size down character and integrity rarely fails me, and Mrs. C. passed my initial scan with flying colors. She sat me down and she reasoned with me instead of shoving garbage down my throat. I learned Hebrew and received my Bar Mitzvah because she was on my side, and because it meant the world to my parents. Personally, ten years later I could still take it or leave it. I am a firm believer that a non-religious person is capable of living a life by a strict moral code whose standard of excellence often stems from a unique perspective on the world. As for myself, I use logic as a guide toward my own idea of what can be considered right or wrong, and through this logic, I follow my own intuitive path rather than relying on what a book of any sort can tell me about being "good". All humans have the capacity to be good, it is just a matter of choice. If religion makes you a better person, than cling to it. If you are killing people in the name of your own idea of what G-d should be, you ought to re-evaluate the foundational principles of your own moral doctrine. I'm not here to declare whether no religion is better than having religion, though we should all be given a choice. Don't you think?

Even to this day I have a hard time taking religious rituals seriously. Last Passover represented the first time I had sat down for this holiday in four years. Ever since I went off to college I had completely disassociated myself from the Temple and even lavished in my freedom to disregard upcoming Jewish holidays as I chose. As tradition dictates during Passover we pass the prayer book around and recognize the four different types of children during the Seder: The Simple Child, The Wise Child, The Wicked Child, and the Child That Cannot Speak. As I am sure the reader can figure, the Wise Child is the suck up who wants to know everything there is to know about Passover, the Simple Child knows not what the ceremony represents but cares to learn more, the Child That Cannot Speak is designated for the young ones at the table, and of course the Wicked Child, well…

The role of the Wicked, irreverent child landed on me. Big surprise. I was the philosopher in the family, the one whose independent mind led him to challenge pre-existing systems of thought and get everyone riled up. Of course I am sure the Torah doesn't see it that way but I took on the role with good humor nonetheless.

Looking back, ever since I was fourteen and no longer had to attend Hebrew School I can accurately pinpoint a real change in myself. The anger subsided and I began to chill out with High School on the horizon. Suddenly I was free every afternoon to hang out with my friends, or watch TV, or do anything I wanted to do. Looking back, even now as a twenty-three year old individual, even after everyone told me I would one day come to appreciate my days in Hebrew school and achieving my Bar Mitzvah, my take on the subject has not changed. I hated it then, and I see it as having little relevance even now. High School was the next phase in my life and gave me the freedom to work toward happiness.

Chapter 4: High School

It was one of the first days of freshman year at Holmdel High School in central suburban, NJ. I sat down next to Rob Pepitone whose house was in the same neighborhood as Max's. I could tell that Rob was more intelligent than the goons we ate lunch with every day. I had friends but I still felt distanced from the masses. Often times at fourteen I would come home after school and sit down in the shower for a good hour or more. I would stay there in a meditative trance until the hot water would start to give. I was escaping to another world. As I began to integrate more socially I found myself doing this less and less. As I write this, it is truly very hard to imagine how I became so socially motivated in high school. Perhaps it was simply excellent follow though, anything to steer away from true introspection, at least for the time being.

Each year of high school after that got better and better. It didn't take us long to discover alcohol in our sophomore year. By junior year I had a girlfriend named Jackie. She was bright and very good looking. I have always had a thing for the brunette model types and Jackie was no exception. We lasted about six months as junior year morphed into senior year and suddenly we all had driver's licenses, cute sophomore girlfriends, and a keg on the weekends. Except for sophomore year when I pulled a 2.3 GPA, my high school grades were solid enough to get into Tulane University, with a little help from the Alumni Association. Only once, during all of high school, did I stop to think about the brilliance of my younger years. Frankly I was having too much fun to care.

Sophomore year was dismal for me academically. Most of my end of the year C's spent a great deal of time in D territory before I finally locked in above 70. By junior year I had picked it up a couple notches. I am not sure how the same inattentiveness and over all nonchalant attitude I had toward academics yielded three decent academic years and one entirely inadequate year. By the end of sophomore year biology class I was so fed up that I raised my hand and asked Mr. Schwartz with a devilishly sincere grin on my face what he would do if I pulled the emergency shower in the back of the class room. He told me as long I was standing right under it and mopped it over afterward it wouldn't be a problem. Mr. Schwartz learned a lesson that day as I stood there in my navy blue surf board shorts and sopping wet white T-shirt, mop in hand.

One day in Mr. Saneki's Psychology class in senior year, I was handed a reminder of my own unpredictability. In the spirit of what is really philosophy instead of psychology, Mr. Saneki handed us all a square piece of paper and told us verbatim, "There is no absolute truth." Immediately I felt a ferocious rush of stimulation. The exercise he had in mind was for each of us to write a short statement, anonymously, in response to his prior statement. I do not think I have ever seen an entire class stupefy in front of my eyes as I did that day. Even the A students in the front of the classroom looked uncomfortable. Looking back it marks the only time I ever felt that stimulative effect in response to a lesson in high school. In response to the question, I wrote impulsively and sloppily with my trusty left hand: IF THERE IS NO SUCH THING AS ABSOLUTE TRUTH, I MUST BE LOOKING AT THE ONLY ABSOLUTE TRUTH. He went through every response out loud. Each response was lamer than the next. My insecurity about being a Jewish kid with what was perceived to be at most average academic abilities caused me to be angry with myself. It was then I realized that this is the type of out-of-the-box thinking the school system ought to further incorporate into the curriculum for kids like me. When he read my answer his jaw dropped as I saw him re-read it just to make sure. He finally muttered, "It's too bad whoever wrote this didn't sign their name because I would have given them extra credit." I raised my hand but I doubt he believed it. He liked me because I was a wrestler but I would have been candidate number 18 or 19 in his mind if he had to speculate as to the author of the response. I don't think any of my teachers thought of me as especially bright with the exception of Mr. Dooley, my AP government teacher senior year. I pulled a B and never took notes…Couldn't take notes…He probably knew I was never paying attention either. I guess that was impressive to him. Really what I had to do was take the book home with me and work hard at self instruction straight from the text.

I used to love Mr. Dooley's class since the course itself was taught at college level and I felt somewhat honored to be surrounded by most of the Asian population in my grade representative of the upper echelon of academic excellence in Holmdel High School. Mr. Dooley was unlike any other teacher I had ever had as his sense of humor kept us laughing almost the whole way through. His Homer Simpson expressions and his random comedic improvisations kept us attentive. A tough task for me but no other teacher had ever been more successful in keeping me engaged. His class was a nice break from the ineffective monotony of the mostly sequential auditory learning style unsuitable for the creative right-brained thinker which was prevalent in the rest of my classes that year, and really every other year including college. He would not only mention the lesson as stated in the text book and transfer it to the blackboard verbatim, but he would actually abstract it in an effort to relate a certain historical event or governmental concept to today's society. I needed more of this to keep me in tune during class, because without a big picture analysis or understanding I am unable to relate to any given lesson and consequently lose interest. This is not to say that I was a perfect pupil in Mr. Dooley's class, as I mentioned my attention span and difficulty with the classroom was just as prominent even inside his classroom. Often times when I am seated and expected to remain in complete attention for the sake of a lecture I am stricken with an almost unbearable urge to get up and move around almost as if to keep my brain alive. I have found, oddly enough, that if I am in motion, my ability to focus during conversation is drastically improved. One day while sitting down in AP Government class as the bell sounded to indicate the end of the period, Mr. Dooley, in an attempt to send me a hint, mentioned to the class that the lesson of the day must have been especially interesting since "Brian" didn't get out of his seat and leave. I deserved the subtle remark as it was true that I would normally leave for about ten minutes a day and wander over to the commons to socialize with my friends in seventh period lunch. The reality of the situation was I needed the break from sitting as most every kid with ADHD has trouble sitting still. Mr. Dooley's was not the only teacher subject to my frequent departures, and often times I'd even be walking around or away without even knowing I was in motion.

Luckily the unbearable urge to get up and move around was provided its own outlet in wrestling practice after school, though, even in the wrestling room there were days where my inattentiveness lead me to some pretty uncomfortable situations. I remember one day in wrestling practice Coach Mullen was teaching us new pin techniques. I was off in Bri Bri Land. I know now that if I was defocused as Mullen gave a physical demonstration of a new technique, there was no chance I was going to catch up when he verbally commanded us to drill. We all knew we were in big trouble if we were having trouble during drilling. He would approach you as he brought the rest of the team to an abrupt halt until the move was performed correctly. I'll never forget the time he stood over me for 45 minutes screaming directions in my face. The rest of the team could only watch as I made the same mistake repetitively. I remember wondering why in the world I could not understand what he was saying. That stung for a couple days but I got over it. My memory of it now is razor sharp: Mullen screaming some sort of foreign language at me whose sound made my ear drums quake and whose content was caught in some sort of echoed feedback loop.

Wrestling overall was a good experience for me as it was able to instill in me a certain physical and emotional confidence that

I have carried with me to this day. Despite my occasional mishaps due to inattention, Coach Mullen was able to bring forth in all of us a new personal peak in mental toughness. We could not possibly have reached this level without his relentless encouragement and in some cases embarrassment and physical pain. It was in the wrestling room where I was able to refine in myself the willingness and wherewithal to stay tough and positive during some of the harder times I went through later on in life. We would run around the high school and middle school twice, the equivalent of about two miles, just to warm our muscles. An extensive stretching session was followed by the actual beginning of practice where Coach would enter the room and begin drilling. If we had performed poorly the night before in a match, or if he was just plain in a bad mood, drilling might be pushed back to make room for a grueling conditioning session usually involving "hit its", a variation of a military training technique where we would have to drop to the floor while simultaneously throwing our legs back into a "V" shape. Other times we would form a line and run around the perimeter of the auditorium scaling up and down the top row seating and into the upper bleachers with fellow teammates on our back.

Senior year was the year I was expected to really make my mark in wrestling as I was prepared in my own mind, and Coach's mind, for a full-time varsity position. I had earned my letter as a junior though I spent a fair amount of time on junior varsity behind some of the seniors who had earned their spot. I was 2-1 early on in the season and had demonstrated remarkable promise before breaking my wrist, for the second time (first time being freshman year), snowboarding at Hunter Mountain in the Catskills region of New York. It was very upsetting for me and disappointing for the team as I watched on the sidelines with a cast up to my elbow for the remainder of my season. As the weather began to turn warm in early spring and my last season of wrestling was behind me, however, I could not have been happier and more carefree. It was almost as if the inner disturbance of the past had completely evacuated. Of course, like most reflective individuals, there was much to think about as college became a reality.

Chapter 5: New Orleans

What better city for a new college student than New Orleans. With an economy that thrives on alcohol consumption and a law system as backward as my scattered mind, I still do not know how that city can possibly be part of the United States. New Orleans was more like a third world country to me, providing me every opportunity to live as reckless and free as I chose. So long as I didn't fail out, which actually was a concern of mine coming in, the next four years would be an immaculate firework display filled with pretty women, mind numbing beverages, and funky music.

When I first arrived my parents took me over to the ERC, or Educational Resources and Counseling Center. Apparently my parents had gone through a lengthy process to qualify me as a special needs student. It was the first I'd heard of it. I suppose the special needs card helped me to get into Tulane but I never really gave it much thought. I was ADHD, big deal right? My first semester course load consisted of Psych 101, Introduction to

Politics, Thomas Jefferson and His Times (my freshman writing requirement), Spanish 101, and Leadership. I ended up dropping Leadership though, as I told my Dad I needed to focus more on my other courses. The truth was I felt outmatched in an interactive classroom of my freshman peers. They were so articulate when they spoke with such an advanced vocabulary. I tried to voice my opinion at one point during the first class but could barely manage to piece together a sentence. I felt like I had some pretty good ideas in my head but I found myself searching for words that did not exist. I remember thinking that those kids were obviously much smarter than me, and I withdrew immediately.

I started thinking maybe the honors dorm was not for me and I began to investigate the two more mainstream dorms, Sharp and Monroe. These dorms were very different from Butler as I noticed right away. They were livelier and much more fun than Butler. These were the kids destined to be the "cool" kids at Tulane. I rationalized a couple days later that they were too "Jappy" for me. I was not used to having any Jewish friends coming from a public high school that averaged somewhere around one Jew per classroom, and frankly I had no affinity toward the Jewish community. Seeing the Jews around campus reminded me of my days in Hebrew School. I felt conflicted about seeing them again. These are the people I supposedly belong to and I had no concept of that. Looking back, the main reason I did not switch out of Butler was because it was intellectually stimulating to me, plus I was beginning to enjoy the interesting individuals roaming the halls. I was living among would be Ivy's that decided a full ride at Tulane might be a nice alternative. These were a great group of people and we had the time of our lives on Butler two that year.

From the beginning Max and I were exploring as usual. We would run up and down the stairwells introducing ourselves to random Butler occupants while pretty much leaving our mark where ever we went. Amber and Robin were nice enough to leave blue markers outside their door for friends to leave notes on their miniature white boards. Clearly they did not mean for me to stay within the parameters of this little square. I wrote in somewhat legible blue marker in gigantic letters, "B-ROB" taking up the entire top half of the door. This was followed by three letters barely legible to the naked eye, "max" The first time I heard B-ROB was the night before and I was digging it. B-ROB soon became its own self manifesting phenomenon. At Tulane I was B-ROB to most everyone who knew me. Later on at Morgan Stanley my colleague, Sizwe coined the term, and it spread like wildfire within my department. I have never once introduced myself as B-ROB but it sure stuck. I think the B-ROB persona even gave me a little leeway for some of the wild stunts I pulled and the overall outlandishness of my personality.

Weeks passed and our first college exams were not far away. I remember our first writing assignment for Jefferson and His Times had already been due. It was a rough draft reflecting on the readings we covered. Since the class was both a history and English class it was our professor's duty to improve our writing while teaching us the important historical perspective as well. He handed us our papers and dedicated the first half of the class to dissecting an anonymous example of what represented the exact specifications of how not to write an introductory paragraph. Of course this paper was mine. Oh well. I was more interested in the brunette who was clearly checking me out from the other side of the table. Her name was Alexia. I always liked the sound of "x" in the name Alexia. It is like the sound of sharp metal object slicing through a block of ice. I would say it is that very sound that encompasses the "friendship" her and I shared until early junior year when I cut her loose.

Max and I used to receive calls almost every night from some fraternity trying to recruit us. We always made a dynamic team. One night we were invited to a party held by the fraternity, PIKE. This fraternity epitomizes the rich-boy, party-hardy mentality of Tulane. These were the northeast city kids who loved women in multiples, excessive quantities of drugs and alcohol, and carried a certain I- don't-give-a-fuck attitude, all of which had major appeal to me. These kids were clearly capable of more mayhem than some of the other primarily Jewish fraternities on Broadway (fraternity row). I was exactly what they wanted as they perceived it. I was good looking, cocky and absolutely craved mind numbing intoxicants of almost any sort. I was certainly the only Butler boy under their consideration.

The party was "Saturate", and I was having a grand old time. We were taking shots of Bacardi that flowed down blocks of ice with chiseled alcohol chutes. At the bottom point we were expected to catch the flow of liquid in our mouths. Later on I was introduced to the Vat" which is Tulane's version of traditional college jungle juice with 190 proof Ever Clear. Of course PIKE was always suspected of adding a little extra something to the mix to help the young ladies relax, but let us not speculate. I remember I found my way upstairs at some point and became part of an unfortunate standstill of movement in the hallway. I was not having nearly as great of a time after the enthusiastic intensity of my initial arrival and I was not sure why. Something about the way these people interacted with each other downright bugged me. I'll never forget when a Paris Hilton type girl cut in front of me with unwavering entitlement as we were all waiting to fill our cups. It was not the act that affected me nearly as much as my awareness of her character. I impulsively dumped whatever was left of my Vat over her artificially glowing blonde hair. It was pure artistic expression if you ask me but I would say her PIKE boyfriend would not agree.

He was one of the upperclassman and therefore not one of the sophomores who were actively involved in recruitment. Once again I was ushered off the premises but this time I was enraged. I recall standing across the street at the corner of where The Boot resides screaming my lungs out for him to come fight me. A couple of the Pikes that did know me came out and offered to buy me some shots as some of the others explained to the upperclassman that they knew me and I was OK. Of course I refused and kept hollering until the NOPD for hire threatened to, "slam my head into the concrete and beat it to a bloody pulp". That was the point where the people I arrived with, including Max, decided it was time for me to move far away from Broadway, at least for the time being. Boy could I be an angry drunk at times. Boy oh boy.

Pike was clearly not for me even though most who knew me probably would have thought differently. I made the decision not long afterward that the mainstream Tulane crown would not be a large part of my life either. Max never wanted to join a fraternity in the first place, but ended up pledging Alpha Tau Omega with me. There were a couple other Jewish guys that fell off the mainstream bandwagon in ATO, which was originally founded as a Christian fraternity. When pledging began I remember being relieved that I passed all my classes the semester prior. I ended first semester with a 2.7 with my best mark in Jefferson and His Times, with a "B". I guess my writing improved despite that dreadful first assignment. The professor told me at one point that it was clear to him that I understood the content of the readings even with some of the poorer papers I handed in. It did take me a while to figure out how to organize my thoughts in such a manner transferable to paper. Later on in life my ideas would flow to paper with great ease.

At the risk of putting ATO through any type of regulatory investigations, I will not go into detail about pledging and all the old anti-establishment ways of a younger Brian in Hebrew school, even though our chapter lost its charter a mere year and a half after I graduated in August of 2005. To sum up my time with pledging, I pissed off many of the older guys by refusing to partake in certain rituals the fraternity religiously abided by, while inviting as much pain and physical punishment that they could possibly administer. I gained respect as a bad ass with a high threshold hold for pain, even though I was clearly putting forth the bare minimum as far as most other organized activities were concerned. There were days when Max and I would come home after a night of boozing and disconnect our phone, knowing full well we were supposed to be at "The House" early the next morning. We did what we wanted for the most part.

By the time sophomore year swung by, I was living with a couple ATO's in an off campus apartment. Max and Danny ended up living together in sophomore housing on campus. They were both offended, but the truth was I needed my own room off campus. One thing I had discovered in college was that I needed a lot of time to myself. Truth is I always manage to offend, in some way or another, anybody who has ever considered themselves to be my friend. I am too independent and capable of connecting with too many different types of people to ever fit within anyone's realm of social expectations. My constant movement allowed me to operate with a certain element of disconnectedness, something that I absolutely needed if I was going to function as one who is social at all. I always wondered how it was possible, for someone who intuitively feels like an extreme introvert, to exhibit such animal magnetism and outward expression. Aside from my friends in the fraternity, I was friends with science geeks, liberal hippies, conservative southerners, and yes, even some Japs. It always amazed me how most everyone else was so one-dimensional in their thinking that they could never be friends with each other. About a month into sophomore year however I could feel this very magnetism and social motivation dim ever so gradually. I never was able to rediscover my social motivation after that point, though after a couple years of what some might call existential depression, the magnetism came back with a sudden spark. More on this at a later time.

It must have seemed funny to a lot of people that I lived with three other ATOs while displaying such a low level of interest in the fraternity's endeavors. My father always told me I was too independent for own good. I found myself reading much more than ever before. I was known to read books here and there but I would never have been described as a bookworm. I am a slow reader as I must visualize what the author is telling me. It is like getting a sneak preview of what a movie based on the book would be like. By early sophomore year, and since that time, there is rarely a time that I can think where I was not reading or studying a book of my choosing. I have always learned more through self study than anything a school curriculum has ever designed, though I was absolutely intrigued by the subject of Philosophy after I took the introductory course second semester freshman year. It was a broad introduction where we heard briefly from classic minds like, Nietzsche, Aristotle, and Socrates.

Philosophy right away struck me as very different from every other school subject I had ever encountered. It had such an innovative appeal to me even though it is ironically the oldest of all academic disciplines. For the many people that disregard philosophy as not necessary or even relevant, I wonder if they ever realized that every other subject in school that they did enjoy is derived from philosophy. True to my nature I still did not read most of the assigned readings but I was never more stimulated by school with just the idea that there are more people like me who are willing to question every convention that stands before them, not to be a pain, but because they need proof in the form of mathematical language. The Philosophical mind is the mind of the true explorer. It is a documented fact that Einstein considered himself a philosopher first, and a scientist second. I began to realize that everything I suspected in one way or another about human character and action was under consideration by some of the greatest thinkers of all time. The very gift that gives me such an eye for the purest kind of sincerity is the very gift of a purely philosophical mind. Finally I was able to appeal to the inner depths of my intellect. I was beginning to look at the way humanity operates in a very different light.

Nietzsche for instance wrote in regards to the will to power that every person supposedly possesses, and being at a school like Tulane, where I was beginning to grow frustrated with the general character of the school's populace, Nietzsche's words manifested into truth. I would contemplate the pressure that was on me to someday become a good Jewish boy and go to business school or law school, and I saw most of the people around me going through those very motions like robots. I began to see myself amongst a group of drones so to speak, making contacts and networking, artificially communicating in order to serve their own selfish agendas.

My perception of human behavior and motives was inching closer to cynical as each day passed. I began to fall into a void of subtle paranoia after what I saw at the time as a major betrayal in trust from someone I had always trusted, this being my best friend, Max. The summer before freshman year, only weeks before we were meant to travel back to New Orleans, he decided to stash a small bag of marijuana in the glove compartment of my Volkswagen without asking my permission. If truth be told, at nineteen years old I probably would have let him ride with it as long as he kept it on his own person but he instead chose to put the entire car load at risk instead, which consisted of the three of us, Max, my old high school friend Terrance, and me. It was a little past 2:00 am on a lazy weekday night, when I made a right on a red light at the corner of Laurel Avenue and Route 35. I barely had time to straighten out the wheel before I saw the flashing red white and blue in my rear view mirror.

The least that could happen, I thought to myself, was the cop would give me a ticket for turning right on red at an intersection that doesn't allow such a maneuver. The officer shined his light in my face and asked me for my license and registration. You see, due to the lack of actual crime in the cozy suburb of Holmdel NJ, the Holmdel Cops figure the best way to spend tax payers money is to focus nearly 100% of their efforts on breaking up house parties and pulling over every other kid with a pair of sideburns and a spoiler on the back of their automobile. I pulled open my glove compartment and there it was, to both my surprise and the cop's, was a bag of weed. All three of us were cuffed as he called for a K9 car to sniff out the rest of my vehicle. Part of me was confused, another part extremely angry, and still another part was somewhat thrilled by the events that unfolded at the end of what seemed to be a rather dull night.

We sat in the station and all I could think about was how Max had let us down, though Terrance and I both figured Max would fess up eventually, thereby doing the right thing. As we left the station and climbed into our friend Adam's car it was mostly silence that consumed us until I lashed out at Max using the full volume of my lungs. I screamed at him, "Why didn't you tell them it was yours? Do the right thing, you didn't even ask me if you could stash your drugs in my car!" He was silent. The days went on and I calmed myself down since the incident while assuring myself that Max was only protecting himself in the station for reasons only the law could make sense of but eventually he would come forth and protect his friends from what was obviously his own mistake. My girlfriend at the time, Allison, who was a Holmdel girl herself, eased me through the tough time by re-enforcing to me that no mother would allow other boys to go down for what her son was ultimately responsible for. Weeks went by however, and Max wouldn't even leave his house let alone talk to me or the group of friends we were both a part of. Max never stepped up, and I don't think I have ever been the same since that incident. Six years later we had gotten past the incident as he assured me that he was trying his best when the sirens were behind us to tell me that there was weed in the glove, but I was too stoned to listen. That might have been the case. Either way it was a shame.

When I came back to Tulane for sophomore year, with summer's incident still fresh in my mind, I began to retreat into myself as I grew disheartened by people I was spending time with. I formulated that if I could not trust my best friend, then I certainly could not trust anybody. Alcohol was still a large part of my life but it began to lose its festive appeal. I needed it to escape as I gather I always have, but the party was over and the road to self destructive behavior was downhill from here. I literally could not socialize without the aid of drugs and or alcohol. Alcohol allowed me to escape while minimizing the anxiety of listening to people speak. The ATO house always welcomed those who wished to intoxicate themselves with no obligation to speak or necessarily be social. Some days I would go to The Boot and grab a seat on the raised platform in the back and watch the mass of people swaying back and forth like a drunken wave pool. It was tough to discern any given individual from the crowd but there was something about my perception that always derived a certain order within what is seemingly chaos. It exists as a purely visual phenomenon and is often accompanied by a rocket ship into Bri Bri Land. I could sit there for hours as the real time image in front of me played with dazzling clarity and overwhelming intensity. What is all this trying to tell me? What is happening that I can no longer play their game as I taught myself in high school?

Meanwhile, Max and I were not talking as a result of both of our arrests and our subsequent falling out. While it was the first time Terrence, Max or I had ever been arrested; it certainly was not my last. Near the end of first semester sophomore year my friend Ben and I took a drunken roller coaster ride at 5am over to the French quarter. I always said that driving drunk in New Orleans was like bowling with those blue inflatable bumpers on the sides of the lane. We caused a ruckus at the Royal Sonesta Hotel on Bourbon Street and ended up in New Orleans Parish County Jail for a solid 14 hour stay.

They took our mug shots soon after we entered into the county jail at which point I gave the camera the middle finger. Once again the NOPD threatened my life but I survived. I still have that picture somewhere. Next thing we knew the sun had risen, or at least it was safe to assume being that there were no windows in our initial holding cells. We were soon ushered into another room down a long corridor and ordered to hand in our clothes and valuables in exchange for a set of Halloween orange Orleans Parish prison apparel. At that point we were ordered to strip to our underwear as Ben and I stood in a line of approximately thirty other individuals as the prison guards scanned our bodies in search of any type of smuggled weapons or other prohibited items. Luckily, for obvious reasons, it was a mass scan rather than the type of individual body search found in airport security, after all, we were merely criminals, not international travelers. In any case, the guards did not do a very good job as Ben and I were almost immediately offered a hit from a lit up joint from one of the young African American individuals to our right. While we both refused, I could not help but feel the slightest sense of admiration for such a bold and ironic move on his part. Though, clearly it was quite stupid at the same time.

Hours passed and we were escorted to another section of the prison where we ended up spending the majority of our stay. The large room had a sort of community feel to it with a large open area in the center where the criminals had the opportunity to walk around and even socialize with one another. Ben and I had entered just as everyone was asked to return to their cells, at which point we were both split up and introduced to our roommates for the time being. I looked over at another young African American individual, representative in my mind as the product of a city whose old south tradition in some way succeeded in repressing the African American Community to the point where the overwhelming dichotomy between the rich and the poor in New Orleans is so drastic that the inevitability of high criminal activity is merely a function of a culturally imbedded and antiquated system, much like the educational system is antiquated. To me, as I sat there in a cell with a man who could be a first degree murderer for all I knew, after all New Orleans and D.C. are in constant competition for murder capital of the country, I merely saw him as human, and no different from myself as we sported the same orange clothes. I looked at him and said, "What's up?" He looked back at me and uttered the same sentiments, "What's up?" And that was that.

I spent the remaining hours in another room with a new group of about thirty people inside the confines of a much smaller area than the initial mass holding cell and this time there was a heavy door rather than bars in-between ourselves and our freedom. We sat there in the midst of a nasty stench with air as thick as gaseous ether waiting for our names to be called. I suppose I deserved all of it. Luckily my friend Danny had bailed me out after a fourteen hour stay and drove me home in his forest green Saturn which he called the "Sex Machine." I spent the duration of the car ride home not thinking about what I had done or how I had ended up in that situation, but rather which bars I was going to hit that night while simultaneously wondering if Ben was going to make it out in time to come with. I was basically un-phased, and furthermore not even scared the least bit at any point during the entire experience looking back. At Tulane this was almost commonplace, as I can think of numerous students aside from myself that ended up staying the night in jail whether it was for underage drinking, which was the most unlikely offense to get busted for in a city like New Orleans, to public urination, which is much more prevalent, and the list goes on. It is like the city of New Orleans issued each of its students a license to make trouble for four years with very little repercussions, though I am not sure any of our parents would agree with such a statement.

When it came to our day in court Ben and I got off with a slap on the wrist thanks to Freddy King, the Tulane Law School educated attorney who is kind enough to lend his services to any Tulane student that finds him or herself in trouble for the meager fee of $250, assuming you didn't kill anyone.

As for myself, and the less than healthy psychology that lead me to such destructive behavior, I suppose part of it was a manifestation of a certain anti-authority attitude I have always carried with me. I never meant any harm to any other human being but there was no denying that sophomore year I was certainly at risk with myself. I was frustrated by losing my best friend in an act of what I saw as utter betrayal at the time, and furthermore I was struggling academically while simultaneously immersing myself into a very philosophical mindset and began, as all amateur philosophers do to some extent before they wisen up , challenging the mindsets of those individuals who in my opinion did not share the same curiosity for life and blindly accepted the environment around them without any real attempt to justify things through appropriate reflection and analysis. I was bitter and relied heavily upon alcohol to merely resolve myself to socialize. I needed help.

Chapter 6: Allie

By second semester sophomore year I was downright angry and paranoid. In classes I still had no capacity to focus. Words carried sound but no meaning and the sentences on the chalk board sometimes had a nearly kaleidoscope- like effect on my eyes but without any aesthetic appeal. I used to walk around with gigantic head phones that reminded me of black plastic ear muffs. They would connect to my Sony disc man with a thick three foot cable manufactured for home stereo systems. Eliza, a girl that lived around the corner from our four room bungalow apartment in what some of my friend's and I would call the "Jap House" told me, somewhat jokingly that she couldn't believe she was friends with the kid who walks around with his head phones on. Of course this was before the IPOD revolution where everyone began walking around with their stringy white ear plugs. Funny how those commercials with the shadow dancer rocking out to his music made it cool and acceptable.

I used to go to class in sweatpants or pajama pants like they were my part of my school uniform. The only time I could be seen in respectable apparel would be around laundry time when all my most comfortable articles of clothing were in desperate need of a wash. I could only clean my clothes with Tide Free or else my skin would get irritated by the harsh chemicals. Often times I would walk into my critical thinking class (Logic 100) with my baby soft black Burton sweatshirt hooded over my enormous black headphones and sit in the back as usual. I didn't utter a word for weeks until the topic of the day was the validation of authority through logistical analysis. My periscope was officially up. I cannot remember what I said so angrily and "brilliantly" at my instructor as I knew he was incorrect, or at least not presenting the full picture, but apparently for the first time, someone took notice in a big way.

Her name was Allie Shapero and she had X-ray vision. She felt my pain like a broken arrow in her heart. All I wanted to know was why did she care? I was clearly not one of the mainstream preppy boys she had been known to rally around and I was not very pleasant to her the couple times I saw her at The Boot or Miss Mae's on Napoleon Ave. One day I essentially told her to get lost and that there was no saving me all the while everywhere I went her beautiful face would be there. The first time we spent time together outside of philosophy class was the night I gladly accepted her invitation to go for a midnight stroll after a drunken night at the Boot. We walked for hours, first down the lemony lit Audubon Drive past a row of beautiful New Orleans style houses and then cut over to the Tulane Green Wave baseball diamond where we had our first kiss in center field. The whole time she was smiling and laughing and squeaking. ROOOBINSOOON!!! She would yell, Step BOY Step! And then she would start dancing to the songs in her head. This girl is as crazy as I am, I remember thinking. She is truly out of her mind and I understood it completely.

During finals week she jittered her way to my apartment as I was half way through the twelve page philosophy paper due the next morning. I had only begun the paper a few hours prior to her arrival but play time always took precedence over work time. We had such chemistry I fear we may have made hydrogen and oxygen jealous. I swung my feet on her lap as she sat on my bed in an effort to get a rise out of her. I knew enough after being with her the last time that bare feet made her squeamish. She instantly took a liking to my feet though, and even took notice of the way my middle toe stuck out longer than my big toe. This was a sign of intelligence according to her and pointed out further that my fingers and hands were that of a surgeon's. My Father is a surgeon I thought to myself, as I shook up the sealed bottle of Schweppes Ginger Ale that I was eyeing from across the room and sprayed her with a blast of fizzy white pop. She laughed and popped her hood up as if to say uncle. We spent the next few hours laughing like little kids all the while my paper remained unwritten. The sun came up and she danced her way back to Sharp Hall on the other side of campus.

That summer we spoke on the phone every other night on average. I was taking a biology class at Seton Hall University marking the beginning of a struggle with a pre-medical curriculum. I'm not sure what it was that possessed me to take calculus, chemistry and physics the first semester back as a Junior, but things were going to change and I vowed to take school seriously for once. I was convinced that the only reason I was a less than stellar pupil for so long was because I was lazy. This was the consensus from my teachers and even my parents as I underachieved year after year from 5th grade through sophomore year in college. I was content with their perception. Underachievement as a description for someone implies a certain amount of unrealized potential. It was much better in my eyes to be underachieving at my level of performance than to be labeled as "doing the best he can". I dreamed that pre-med would be cake if I actually paid attention in class and studied like some of the others on campus. What did it matter that I had never taken a high school physics class or a pre-calculus class and had never taken any the pre-requisites?

Allie came over one evening as I was staring blankly at chapter one in my Chemistry text book. My new and improved attitude regarding paying attention in class was enjoying about as much success as the inauguration of Euro Disney. Paying attention was not a choice I soon determined, and I resorted to self study as I spent each class on a new adventure in "Bri Bri Land" If only the educational system built for the masses, the very system that has time and time again denied the genius of would be scientific and entrepreneurial pioneers, had seen the LD that I later identified in myself, my trend of tiresome underachievement and academic struggle would have instead opened the door to a real sense of accomplishment. But let us not speculate on the bygones of yesterday and focus our efforts on the inattentiveness of today. Allie could see the anguish on my face as the chemical equations in front of me were burning my eyes. She popped a blue colored pill in my mouth and told me, "Here, try this"

Adderall by that time was passed around on most college campuses as if they were nothing more than "skittles". I had long ago given up on medicine to help tame my ADD but this stuff was different. My thoughts began to flow with water like lucidity and I could stare at a textbook for hours without fatiguing. The one myth about Adderall is quickly debunked though. It does not make one smarter; it simply helps to harness the imbedded intelligence one already possesses in a more productive manner. Despite all the studying I was doing however, I was doomed from the start when it came to Pre-med. My less than stellar grasp of simple algebra did not help me on my first physics exam as I scored a dismal fifteen percent. Meanwhile I simply could not juggle Chemistry and Calculus on top of my intermediate level philosophy class at the time. My frustration grew deeper as my relationship with Allie became more serious by the passing minute. It has always been in my nature to impulsively take on more than I can handle. Part of this stems from the impulsiveness of ADD but the rest comes always wanting and desiring things for the moment.

I recall spending a weekend with my parents early fall semester of junior year in Arizona. My parents were there to golf but were thrilled none- the- less to accommodate their stressed out son. My Dad and I sat down and plowed through five hours of physics, of which the first couple hours consisted of a basic algebra tutorial. The concepts involved in physics were not a problem for me; I simply did not know algebra from Arabic. It was always very frustrating to me that I felt I could always manage an intuitive grasp of scientific concepts but I simply lacked the ability to calculate numbers. I later learned that this sort of thing is typical for a visual thinker like me. I am able to visualize concepts with much depth but often times two plus two equals five after overanalyzing. I felt so stupid. Allie would reassure me time and time again about how brilliant I truly was, which only intensified my embarrassment at the substandard grades I pulled all semester. I used to wonder when she was going to realize that I was a complete fraud. My plan was in ruins as finals came around and all the studying I did yielded a mere 2.5 for the semester. I managed a C in physics, a B in chemistry, and a withdrawal from calculus.

The next semester, in typical non-sequential form, I decided I was ready to take genetics in front of its prerequisite, Cell Biology 101. If rote memorization and the commitment of raw detail coupled with neglect of a big picture perspective is my weakness, then genetics looking back was a mistake from the beginning. I came through with a C- while digging myself into an even deeper hole. My grade point average plummeted to 2.4 from 2.7 by the end of junior year yet I continued to study pre-med. I made the decision that the Universidad de Guadalajara would be my future medical school as all the American medical schools had been more than ruled out by my own incapacity to study effectively. It is one thing, as I touched upon earlier, to walk through life with the comfort of knowing that there was always unrealized potential whose actuality never materialized due to one's own inability to spawn the necessary motivational force, but it is a completely different situation when one tires themselves through tortuous preparation, only to fail in the end. I am not sure which is worse.

Allie and I were in another realm from the beginning and the depth and intensity of our love was more than either of us could handle in college at the time. Allie lived with three of her friends no more than a block from where I lived junior year on 700 Broadway. Her charisma and class along with her high voltage personality made her not only popular, but a leader. She was not like the rest of the Tulane girls that followed her every move. For one, she did not have an eating disorder which really made her stand out among the "in" crowd of Tulane socialites, at least in my eyes. Her dedication to yoga kept her in great shape. She was the bearer of sage advice and a lover of all that was fun and exciting on the Tulane campus. She was also lost in a world of superficiality and vanity, and she knew it didn't suit her despite her irrefutable ability to take center stage. The life I had pledged junior year, to be an introverted pre-med student represented a proposition of stunning polarity as we both retreated into our relationship while the rest of the world stayed its course. Allie used to say, in true Shakespearean form, that "love is the sweetest of dreams and the worst of nightmares." We fought amidst the peer pressure her friends would lay on her in heavy doses to party with them, and amidst my own seemingly futile effort to succeed in my classes, and yet we loved each other dearly.

We ended up taking numerous weekend trips to get away from it all. There was the time we crossed through the barren yellow of Mississippi only to stop at the official motel of the SS Alabama outside Mobile, AL. The motel was like any other motel in the nation with the exception of a giant Navy Submarine docked right outside. Another time we took a trip to Houston, Texas to catch a country music concert at Minute Maid stadium, formally Enron stadium before the awful accounting scandal. We used our fake IDs to get in since the bars weren't carding inside. I drank like a fish to drown out the inbred sound of a musical genre I was still far from accepting at the time. She took the first leg of the ride home while I sobered up. It marked one of the very few times she was allowed to drive my car in any situation, but it just was not worth it for me to drive under the influence in a state that thrives on rodeos and capital punishment. We were about 50 miles outside Houston when Allie decided to drive on the left lane of a two way street. We swerved out of the way of a car and ended up on the muddy shoulder of the right side of the road as she hit the brakes and we hydroplaned off a 4 foot launching pad of uneven landscape and glided to a complete stop as the giant VW emblem met violent acquaintance with an unassuming telephone pole. Luckily we both emerged unharmed. We flew home complements of Allie's generous father the next day.

While there is much more to say about the magnificently brilliant and beautiful Allie Shapero I must move on as we will hear from her throughout the rest of the story. I credit Allie for much of what I have become today. She planted the seeds of confidence in me during some of the tougher times of my existence, and they are just now beginning to show themselves in the form of growth and expansion. I dropped pre-med second semester senior year with only two classes remaining, Physics 2 and Chemistry 2, which I had failed once before. Somehow I found my way through Organic Chemistry 1 and 2 with a D and a B respectively. I graduated the summer following the spring that most of my 2005 peers graduated, following the long anticipated completion of calculus. Max is still living the Tulane lifestyle to this day as he comes closer to graduating himself. Allie was off to Prague for the final semester of her college career and I was off to Shanghai, China as part of a work study type program I had been accepted into midway through senior year. It was time to get away for a while.

Chapter 7: Vision Asia

As part of a two chapter tribute to the emerging economic super power that is the expansive land of China, I must begin with a brief summation of the events that lead to my departure in September of 2005. Allie and I were taking an anthropology class, Modern Chinese Society in the spring semester of my senior year. Allie had always embraced eastern philosophy and practiced Yoga on an almost daily basis. She was very talented and even encouraged me to take Kung Fu classes where I eventually earned my Blue Belt. Our class was taught by a Miss Du who had written a book based on her extensive experience in the cultural transformation China had undergone since the post Mao communist regime. While significant change had already transpired in China long before its widespread coverage in the United States, my decision to travel to Shanghai, China was cutting edge for the time, as there is always a significant lag between that of major change, and the mass recognition of such change, especially in this country.

Most of what I knew about China had derived itself from all the martial arts movies I had seen. My all time favorite was the aesthetically dazzling and philosophically inspired, "Hero". It remains one of my all time favorite movies to this day, tied with "Gladiator". It depicts a character whose family was slaughtered by the Emperor's imperial army on its road to a unified China. At the time China was fractioned into sovereign providences, though the power of the Emperor's army was growing exponentially despite the resistance of the land. The main character swore revenge and drew up an elaborate plan to physically situate himself close enough to the Emperor, disguised as a loyal follower. Our hero was the only martial artist in the land with the ability to execute the type of deadly attack necessary to dethrone and assassinate the Emperor, and by the time the Emperor realized his mistake, the pieces were already in checkmate. Hero did not follow through with his plan as he looked into the king's heart and was reminded of a friend he met along the way whose notion of "Our Land" rang true in his soul for the first time. Suddenly unification became the roadway to a glorious future for the Chinese people, according to his untimely revelation, as our Hero died for his effort in the face of a compassionate, yet, pragmatic Emperor.

Like the United States after it, a country that stands for unity while paying homage to the sum of its parts will ultimately reap the benefits of a global leadership in thought and influence. General Sun Zhu, author of the internationally known, Art of War, advocated that one must know his enemy in order to conquer, while one must know himself in order to be unconquerable. Countries must know themselves and their enemy as this very principle is universally proportional. Our schools must recognize the brilliance of those lateral thinkers whose learning style remains variant from those of the norm within the school system. In the utilitarian point of view of our nation's school system, the education that maximizes the amount of students who benefit from a particular learning style, are ultimately responsible for minimizing the potential of the truly brilliant minds that have the most to contribute to society. As it follows, maximizing the mass of students who benefit from our countries educational system, DOES NOT MAXIMIZE THE GOOD OF THE MASS OF SOCIETY. History has proven time and time again that it is the mind of just one individual whose independent ideas prove to be the catalyst of cultural or scientific progression. We must know ourselves in order to reverse this trend of neglecting that which is truly brilliant in our schools, and we must know our enemy in the form of that which stands in the way of competing on the global stage of intellectual progress.

When I first arrived at Shanghai Pu dong airport the first thing I noticed in this great land of economic and scientific innovation was the foreign pictographic symbols of the Chinese language. I silently prayed that the mass influx of westernization and transformation in this country would give way to English subtitles on street signs, at least in Shanghai, the thought leader in Chinese economic pioneerism. As we landed the stewardesses were kind enough to inform us as to where we could pick up our baggage. Of course my mind was elsewhere and the words deflected off my skull like ping pong balls. I spent a good hour trying to locate my baggage after many failed attempts to engage in conversation with some of the baggage handlers. Finally I saw three red pieces of luggage sitting by their lonesome that looked familiar.

I grabbed them and met with David, the director of the program. He introduced himself as we packed his car up in anticipation of the two hour crawl through traffic into the heart of Shanghai. As early evening gave way to night, I was genuinely exhausted after the fourteen hours of flying I had just endured. I recall being hypnotized by the electronic map that we each had on the back of the headrest in front of us. While everyone else was watching Seinfeld or Mr. and Mrs. Smith with Brad Pitt and Angelina Jolie on their personal screens, I was too busy watching in awe as we were literally flying over the North Pole before we dipped down through Russia, Mongolia, and then China. There were little icicles forming on the windows as we rounded the top of the globe and now there were blindingly exuberant neon lights keeping me awake as we passed through the outer circumference of the famous Pu Xi (East) region of Shanghai. Shanghai is truly a sight in the night time as most of the major buildings are lit up in celebration of themselves as the thriving economic drivers of a newly emerging city in the midst of one of the grandest economic revolutions in world history. Everything was changing before my very perception, and the United States was still a good year away before fully appreciating the magnitude of the seismic shift in global influence that lay ahead. Picture a collection of highly energetic molecules aggregating in the early phases of a big bang, or on a simpler note, picture yourself as you watch from the stands as a high school freshman named Lebron James lights a gym up with 40 points in nowhere in Ohio; The early phases of a global phenomenon.

That first night we sat down and enjoyed a traditional schezuan dinner complete with spicy peanut chicken, thinly sliced pork, dumpling soup, and for dessert, a community bowl of oversized tapioca balls drowned in warm sugary water. To my left were Zach and Tiffany, two 30 year olds who dropped everything to spend three years in Shanghai. Tiffany was fresh out of the Georgetown MBA program while Zach was a graduate of Wharton Business School with five years of investment banking under his belt. They were newlywed as of the previous July, and with Zach being Cantonese and Tiffany being a blonde Midwesterner from Indiana, they were certainly an interesting duo from the start. To my right was Angela, a quiet Chinese girl from Los Angeles with a cool demeanor and an anxious desire to please. She sat quietly as

David, the program director enlightened us with such details as to where we could find phone cards to call home, proper attire for our internships, as well the current Yuen to Dollar currency exchange ratio, which was somewhere around 8: 1 at the time of my arrival.

Following dinner David showed Angela and I to our hotel which was situated approximately 20 minutes subway ride to Peoples Square, and 30 minutes from the famous tree lined French Concession of Shanghai. The Xin Yu In Hotel boasted a friendly staff with a nicely maintained lobby and elevators that operated with excruciating slothfulness. For a city that seemed to be riding a bolt of lightning to the frontier of technological innovation, how in the world could an elevator function with such disregard to the times? Our rooms were no less retro with their neon yellow bed covers and bright pink desk lamps, it felt like sleazy Miami disco of the late 1970's. And boy was it hot! Shanghai in early September was as hot and offensively humid as New Orleans. I recall laying there that first night, having not seen Allie since she left Tulane after the first summer session of classes had ended in early July, and thinking that times certainly were changing unrecognizably. Part of me embraced this idea, as I have always chased after exotic new experiences, but there was something about the blinding yellow of my bed sheet that sent me off to sleep with an unwavering sense of depression in my gut.

The next morning I was up by eight with my Nike air maxes laced up tight for what I could feel was going to be a very long walk. I knew nothing about the geography of Shanghai aside from their signature television tower that looks more like a radioactive rocket ship ready to take off for the planet Techno Rave. Dating back to as early as I can remember, with particular emphasis on the numerous hours I used to spend exploring the wilderness of Holmdel and Toms River, I have never hesitated to point myself in a seemingly arbitrary direction with nothing but self-guided instinct as my compass. My destination was the waterfront where the TV tower would inevitably be found and all I had with me was my honed spatial intuition for direction. I found myself walking down roads whose names I could not pronounce even with the English subtitles. I remember stopping for a cold bottle of green tea at a convenience store. The cost was 3 Yuen, or close to 40 cents. After about a mile and a half of walking I saw what struck me as a faint outline of the television tower I had only seen in pictures on the internet. Judging by the fleeting vista of tall buildings and more importantly the TV tower in the distance, and my own relative geometric positioning, there were clearly hours of undiscovered city to cover before my mission would be complete.

I walked past neighborhood after neighborhood of the most efficient looking apartment complexes that seemed to multiply with every passing day as thousands more Chinese move to Shanghai in search for a more prosperous existence. I found myself at one point on a dirt paved alley way that might as well have been 300 years back in time as I passed by men selling live chickens from cages and families tending to their stock of live snakes and other unidentifiable river specialties, as if they were tending to a new shipment of the latest DVD player to hit the market, which was a significantly more common sight in the tech savvy world of Shanghai consumerism. Old neighborhoods like the one I found this first day are truly the hidden gems of a rapidly westernizing city whose ancient Chinese culture has dissipated into the thick cloud of industrial smog that monopolizes the air passages of inexperienced tourists. Two hours later I found myself on the Huang Pi river front gazing toward the western portion (Pu Dong) of Shanghai. Present was the ever expanding financial district which crowded around the colossal Jim Mao tower, the tallest and most modern looking building in Shanghai. It reminded me of the way the Empire State building looks nestled amongst the hundred or so other smaller buildings in New York City, as one could only view it across the Hudson River from New Jersey. Of course, last but not least, the most uniquely designed television tower, with its syringe like body beaded with two massively rotund neon balls, as only the Chinese could draw up, stood before my very eyes like an over grown tripod on acid.

I taxied it back to the hotel since there was no plausible method to retrace my steps. It is one thing to point yourself in the general direction of a giant back drop and strut your way through an urban obstacle course of random confusion. It is an entirely different scenario to even attempt to reverse the process. It is like anything, the more non-linear an approach utilized in reaching toward a goal, the more chaotic a process becomes until we have reached the point of irreversibility. This is universal entropy at its finest, and hence, my justification for hailing a taxi. On another note, I was plain beat. The Shanghai taxis are lined with white seat covers for an extra touch of sophistication as one is driven through this utter freak of a city. If a passenger does not know the Chinese language, he better have a card with a written address for the driver to read. Of the hundreds of Taxis taken in my four months living in Shanghai, I can only count one time where my driver could manage more than a "Hello". They were truly their own breed, with their thermoses filled with loose leafed green tea, and their routine near death collisions around every bend, the Shanghai taxi drivers made New York taxi drivers seem laid back.

A couple nights later the program set up a dragon boat tour down the Huang Pi River for the whole group of Abroad China interns. It was that very night that I met Ahmad Mohtadi, the Saudi born Sheik of Miami Florida. I could tell right away that Ahmad and I were going to be spending a lot of time together. For starters, we figured out quickly that he was my next door neighbor back at the hotel, and he could clearly hold his own in the drinking department as well, judging by the way he guzzled his first Tsingtao beer. The boat docked and we hit the town. First it was the white lights and glitziness of Tong Reng Lu (Lu is road in mandarin). Tong Ren Lu was just down the road from the Shanghai Ritz Carlton and a short walk from the newly constructed Shanghai Convention center where business men flock to introduce their latest product into the China market. Ahmad and I took 3 shots of Jameson Whiskey and stood as two lone gunmen since the last of the interns had long ago said their goodnights and farewells. We hopped in a taxi and ended up on Chu Lu Lu, where we were told we would find the last of the open bars. Within minutes we found ourselves slumped over on bar stools playing connect four with the lady bartenders alongside a drunk English expatriate and his lovely Shanghainese girlfriend.

What a night.

After an interesting weekend it was time to get ready to work. Upon acceptance to this program Abroad China sent my resume to a multitude of Chinese companies looking for English speaking interns. Jamie Gwyn, managing director of his own consulting company, Vision Asia, also happened to be a Louisiana State graduate and jumped at the chance for a Tulane kid to work among his entirely Chinese staff. Jamie arrived in Shanghai in 1999 under the pretense that he would perform potato logistics for Frito Lay. He recognized potential in a growing, though very immature Shanghai market when he arrived and opened up his own shop. When I arrived in 2005, Vision Asia was in the process of being merged into a larger and more knowledgeable Spire Research and Consulting. I realized immediately that the fledgling enterprise called Vision Asia had nothing to offer its clients. I walked in with Tiffany, who had also been selected to Vision Asia as we were greeted by a very amiable and somewhat nervous Belinda Yu. Belinda was born in Beijing and spoke English with an Australian accent. She and the rest of the Vision Asia work force were especially cheery and welcoming. In Shanghai they are putting forth their best effort to acclimate themselves toward a westernized model of business and employing true blooded Americans was a sign of prestige and dominance. My greatest tangible asset in Shanghai coming out of college with a liberal arts degree was not my diploma, but merely the fact that I could speak English in a rapidly adapting Chinese business world. Tiffany and I were celebrities.

After Belinda provided us with a brief overview of what was expected from us, Jamie walked through the glass door of the conference room and introduced himself. Jamie is 5'5 at most, which figured him to be about average among Chinese males but on the short end of the spectrum by American standards. I had a solid 4 or 5 inches on Jamie easily, while Tiffany's 6 foot height downright towered over Jamie. He told us right away about how exciting a time is was to be experiencing Shanghai and he couldn't be more right. I could feel the cities' undercurrent of energy and growth with every stride. It was amazing to me how Jamie, or any western entrepreneur could own and operate his own company in China and not know more than a couple sentences of mandarin. Even in their own country, a Chinese individual must learn to speak the language of the American busines man if they have any aspirations of being more than a farming peasant or a low grade urban service provider. In hindsight this concept suited my auditory issues superbly. No matter how many times I would ask someone at work to repeat themselves, short of Jamie and Tiffany, they automatically assumed it was their own broken English that was the problem instead of my processing issues.

Following Jamie's introduction we all took a walk through the French Concession and sat down for a fancy Schetzuan style lunch. All the staples of a westernized Chinese food takeout meal were present as we nibbled on Kung Pao Chicken and spare ribs. Things became interesting however, when the waiter brought out frogs legs, which I of course tried. My philosophy on food is I will try anything at all if it is edible. My curiosity is too much to bear when it comes to new adventures. After the frog's legs we were all enticed by a fried jelly fish, though the most unexpected dish of the afternoon appeared in the form of a white tofu like substance in a black cauldron over a small flame. The flame was responsible for a subtle boiling of a dark red liquid upon which the white cubes resided in a somewhat submerged manner. Instinctively I reached for a piece of what I thought to be tofu and slid it into my mouth, grinned and swallowed. Oscar, Jamie's right hand man wanted to know right away how I had enjoyed what was probably my first taste of boiled pig's blood. I told him I enjoyed it very much and would like some more.

As weeks passed I had already grown weary of my job. I was under Oscar's supervision as I was expected to create a power point presentation based upon some of the research the other Chinese employees had gathered for the Shanghai market for document management. Oscar's English was so poor and his directions so imprecise that I had supposedly been working for two weeks on a project whose comprehension was somewhere in the Pacific Ocean between Hawaii and Japan. While it was true that I had not the slightest idea of the directions Oscar gave me, my abilities to pick up on the conceptual structure of a situation beyond the spoken word informed me rather quickly this project was founded upon a less than cogent methodology. The research I was handed pertaining to Fuji-Xerox printer/fax machine lineup lacked real insight as it consisted of information that any individual could easily extract from the company's website in a matter of twenty minutes. I was in a standstill until Jamie called me into his office sometime in late September and suggested that Oscar and I were perhaps not sharing in a productive working relationship. I impulsively responded with the notion that if Oscar truly had a problem that he take it up with me personally. In the United States, if two men have a problem with each other, they resolve it face to face. This idea is attributable to the working world as well as beyond it. Jamie agreed with a somewhat genuine gesture of affirmation, though he was not overwhelmingly moved.

The next day I was moved over to Sales where poor Tiffany had been cold calling virtually every Chinese company with a Shanghai, Beijing, or Hong Kong area code in an effort to drum up business. The goal was to obtain the address of a given company's head of marketing and send them a packet of information regarding the glorious things Vision Asia could do for them. While I was not really enjoying myself with my power point presentation on fax machines, I downright pitied Tiffany after listening to weeks of her futile attempts in pitching an empty product to "actual" profitable companies. I was fuming when Jamie decided to transfer me to

sales as I knew I could not possibly go through with dialing all day.

I took a break upstairs in an unfinished part of the building that was

beginning to turn into a daily refuge of mine. I called Allie to

unwind. My anger got her riled up as she understood all too well my

problem with the situation and listened as I said my piece. She told

me she loved me and to suck it up and I walked back downstairs a

bit calmer than before. It was true, even when cold calling, that

fluent English from the mouth of an American was instantly

recognizable and matched with respect, but it was not enough to

engage the vast majority of executives with a less than novel idea

and product for very long.

The job was sliding down a sharp declining slope as far as

priorities were concerned. Shanghai to me was just another

playground and would pick up nicely where I left off at Tulane.

Bourbon Street Hand Grenades and dollar Jack and Cokes became

Blueberry Mojitos and Chivas Regal on the rocks as Ahmad and I

came home to the Xin Yu in lit up like a full Shanghai moon every

night. Our favorite place to rendezvous was the internationally heralded, Bar Rouge, which was situated right on the Bund with the most fantastic view of Pu Dong in all of Shanghai. We would get blitzed on the rooftop of a gorgeous seven floor building with a muscular stone façade among a crowd of incredibly good looking western expats who did not think twice about paying 5 times the going rate for a beer in Shanghai as long they were able to enjoy it among the city's most elite party scene at Bar Rouge. I recall vividly as I open the media player in my mind, the blazing electricity of the Shanghai (Pu dong) skyline as viewed from the Bar Rouge patio at night. The eccentric neon colors would flash rhythmically throughout the night as if they were begging for the rest of the world to start paying close attention. I would sit in a hypnotic trance as the lights tickled the inner sensory mainframe of my mind with sharp potency. The flapping of the red and yellow Chinese Flag above me would signal my subconscious with high frequency anticipatory vibrations of new era.

Back at work the excitement was building up for the Chinese Moon Festival on the first week of October. Moon Cakes, which are best described as disc shaped coffee cakes offered in a vast array of interesting flavors such as red bean, or egg yolk, were as abundant as skittles and Milky Way bars around Halloween time in the States. Since the holiday allowed for an extended weekend I took the opportunity to secure a ticket to Prague to see Allie. My mother is really a wiz with some things, and luckily, the optimal usage of frequent flier miles happens to be one of her specialties. Since the trip was somewhat last minute and nearly over booked she managed to reserve a remaining first class ticket for me on route to Paris. Ahmad and Angela were helping me pack my red carry-on luggage when Angela took a quick glance at my passport and she all of the sudden seemed slightly amused and thoroughly baffled. She had figured out ten minutes before I was scheduled to leave for the airport that my Chinese visa was only single entry. The three of us debated this new revelation for some time before I decided that I would just have to deal with the problem at the Chinese Embassy in Prague. In my life I have been described as lawless many times and this was one of those times where I could certainly understand such an assessment. When it comes to red tape rules and meaningless regulation, I have been known to be unashamedly noncompliant. My flight took off that night from Shanghai Pudong airport.

I watched the digital map as we flew northwest from Shanghai, through Beijing and then Mongolia. I fell asleep around the time the plane began to point due west over Russia. When I awakened my vision was instantly drawn to the lights below, which according to the map was the city of Warsaw. Russia soon transitioned into Eastern Europe as we flew against the earth's rotation and faster than the rising sun behind us. When we landed in Paris it was still a couple hours before daylight. I had never been to France and did not have any desire to stay longer than necessary. From what I have heard about the French people they are largely Anti-American and Anti-Semitic. I found it fascinating how my experience in their airport stood in considerable contrast to this notion as I barley had to alter my stride as long as my American Passport was visible. When we walked off the plane I flashed my passport to the French officers as they were busy giving a Chinese traveler from my flight a hard time. They searched through his entire luggage while to my surprise, the Chinese traveler voiced a calm but stern protest in reference to the injustice he thought himself to be experiencing at the time. I distinctly recall him telling the officers that he would only show them respect if they showed him respect in turn. Since I was in constant motion, it was of course simple to process the entire conversation.

We were well on our way to Prague as I engaged myself in a short conversation with the gentleman sitting next to me. From the English I heard him utter to the stewardess I could tell he was American, which felt somewhat foreign to me having just taken off from Paris and before that, Shanghai. He told me the company that employs him sends him all over Europe to handle factory integrations as they continue to expand their global presence. He didn't offer any more details but he did mention that he missed his family very much. I thought of my family too. My mom had expressed over one of my last dinners with my family before leaving for Shanghai that she didn't think I was coming back. As we landed in Prague I wondered the same thing. I had been struggling to find a suitable fit for myself occupation wise, and since Med School was certainly not feasible, the only other options for a "good Jewish boy", or so I thought at the time, were basically limited to Law School or Finance of some sort. I never understood how people could simply flock to law school in herds without even a glimmer of an idea of what they stand for. As far as I was concerned the large majority of students in law school didn't have a clue what they are doing there aside from the promise of a potential six figure salary and a pat on the back from their parents, or a rabbi. On top of that, Corporate America epitomized the cookie cutter herd mentality that I have always been so opposed to. I truly had a lot to work out in my mind, but for the time being my focus happily diverged to the thought of seeing Allie.

Immigration was fairly painless and I had no problem withdrawing 1000 Koruna's. One Yuan was valued at approximately 2.75 Koruna's. My 40 minute taxi into Praha cost me about 500 Koruna's, or 25 dollars give or take. In truth all the necessary monetary conversions and paper work involved in international travel really didn't strike me as all that difficult to manage, and by 22 years old, the intensely visual world I had grown accustomed to would simply melt into a new frame with stunning cinematographic mastery. I am told it was not always that way for me, especially when I was a young boy but somewhere along the lines I had learned to emotionally embrace the uncertainty of Chaos rather than resist it. As I was driven through the rural in-betweenness of the airport and the city I was rather absorbed in the density of Prague's aura. Its coloring reminded me of the dusty pastel chalk that little kids scribble on elementary school playgrounds, only there was clearly nothing playful about it. The city carried a think emotional undertone, possibly as a result of the Velvet Revolution and recent turnover from communism to capitalism.

Allie kept asking me the next day as we walked through the city, "How do you like my Little Praha?" It really was where she belonged, at least for a period of time. Prague is like a living fairy tale with a castle on top of a hill overlooking the city and enough pink and purple to make any imaginative girl crown herself Princess of the land. We walked all day with no particular destination in mind as we absorbed the majesty of one of the few preserved cities that went virtually untouched during World War Two. She would attend class until early afternoon while I roamed around with my new digital camera that I had purchased impulsively in Shanghai and took some beautiful shots of the city until Allie and I met up later. We had dinner the next night with a couple of her friends at an Italian restaurant near the center of town and found ourselves at a somewhat rundown bar for the remainder of the night. To my eager surprise there was a bottle of Absinthe, the legendary hallucinogenic alcohol banned throughout most countries. I took shots with two of Allie's buddies from the program, one of which I was sure had a crush on her. The taste can best be described as a mixture of a Listerine like mintyness combined with a package of liquefied black liquorish and moonshine. It was harsh but still went down better than some tequila. The absinthe did not do the trick as far as I was concerned.

By the third day in Prague I realized that something had to be done about my little Chinese visa problem. I took a taxi to the Chinese embassy in Prague and found my way in through a back entrance. There was but one cranky Czech woman tending the front desk while the rest of the department took the week off in honor of the moon festival. She informed me that if I had tried yesterday they would be able to accommodate me, but there was nothing that could be done for me at this point. I chuckled to myself as I was used to this type of thing by now, and 99% of the time things magically work out for me anyway. I theorized that the Chinese embassy would let me in regardless of one minor lacking detail such as a double entry visa. As I stood in the airport line in Prague it was very difficult for Allie and I to say goodbye. We had always been better together than apart and despite the fact that it did take a little while to for us to get back in rhythm; by the end of my trip we were living a dream. She asked me to stay with her, though I knew that was not an option for me.

I took off for Paris and from Paris to Shanghai. I sat next to a wealthy looking Arab individual looking to be about my age in first class on route to Shanghai. He was one of those Europeanized Arabs with his diesel sneakers and artsy metrosexual attire. We exchanged a few words and both ended up sleeping most of the way back. As we stood in the two hour long bloated catastrophe of an immigration line somehow I ended up a good twenty people in front of him as I finally found myself only a few feet from the passport check point. I nodded at him as they called my name and subsequently forfeited my travel documents to the female immigration officer in true nonchalant, Brian fashion. She eyed my passport with robotic precision and called my bluff within seconds. Unphased, I figured I would pay a fine of some sort and the situation would dissolve into itself. She called upon an armed security officer and I was ushered down a white hallway into a back room. The whole scenario spawned an image in my mind of an American soldier in Vietnam being whisked away by his communist captors for an unfortunate torture session. While I knew this was not actually the case, I did realize that the severity of the last couple of minutes probably should have put me at some degree of uneasiness but instead I couldn't be more amused. Looking back it is these types of situations that made me feel alive. Similar to the way I felt after I had jumped out of a plane with Max and a couple other guys from my fraternity a few years back, or to the many instances where Allie and I would crash our skulls together with full force as a ringing reminder to our brains that we exist.

I was having the time of my life as the Chinese officer informed me that I was going to be deported. Ahmad had called me at that very moment and asked me when I was coming back to the Xin Yu Inn so we could hit the bars. I gave him the low down. Basically my options were to fly back to Paris where I came from and allow Air France to incur the $800 penalty in addition to cost of airfare for their failing to check my visa prior to my departure for Shanghai, or I could fly to Hong Kong and pay the penalty on my own dollar. Ahmad advised that I fly to Hong Kong and take care of business there and I concurrently agreed. While I did consider flying back to Paris and eventually to Prague to take Allie up on her offer to stay with her for the rest of her semester abroad, I knew I would ultimately be shortchanging myself with such a course of action. I handed my Platinum American Express card with the name Brian J Robinson printed on the front to initiate a transaction that in actuality, would end up billing Neil H. Robinson. When I arrived in Hong Kong I made sure to email my father and recommend that he deduct $1000 from my account in light my most recent adventure. He did.

I woke up early in the bed of my airport hotel bedroom in order to make sure my one full day in the city of Hong Kong did not go to waste. I walked through the hotel lobby and down a connecting escalator to the airport's main floor. I quickly honed in on the desk in charge of issuing visas to mainland China. Hong Kong is actually a subtropical island located off the Southeastern shore of the mother country. While the British did secede their governmental rights to the once imperially ruled Hong Kong at the turn of the century, from an economic standpoint Hong Kong is considered a sovereign territory. As an international financial powerhouse they do not wish to make the travel of a Western Businessman any more arduous than the full day of travel already entailed in a voyage to the south pacific and fortunately for me an American passport would suffice upon entrance to Hong Kong. The individuals at the desk were very helpful as they informed me my reentrance visa would be available the following morning and even recommended a hotel I could stay in for less than half of what I paid the night before. I exchanged my Koruna's for Hong Kong dollars, which are more or less equivalent in value to the Yuan and caught the next monorail for a 40 minute Disneyesque ride into the heart of Hong Kong. I then took a complimentary bus to a lovely hotel whose Chinese name escapes me.

I threw my bag full of what was not entirely dirty laundry into my room and walked outside with the map of the city that I received upon check in. Hong Kong was clearly very different from Shanghai, I remember observing. While they are both somewhat dirty there was a level of sophistication present in Hong Kong that one would expect to find in a city whose identity has already been established. There is no denying the immensity of the grandeur that is Shanghai, but it is a young city in the midst of an overly exuberant adolescence. There was also an undeniable British influence in Hong Kong as all the cars were equipped with steering wheels on the right side and the architecture of some of the fancier 5 star hotels I walked past were more stately and classically old fashioned in design than most of the overly energetic decadence one would find in Shanghai. There was no mistaking that I was still in China, however, as there was no shortage of pesky street salesman trying to peddle their latest pirated copy of Sin City on DVD or a brand new 2 cent Rolex. After a couple hours of exploring I ended up at the water front gazing at all the fishing

boats streaming through the river at a sea turtle-like pace. Hong

Kong certainly was not in any rush like Shanghai, I remember half

thinking as I parachuted down from Bri Bri land.

I decided I would return to the waterfront at night. I knew

from the map I had scanned briefly that the Hong Kong Science

Museum with an IMAX theatre was not far from the point at which

I was standing. I have been to my share of science museums back in

the States and figured it would be interesting to see the Chinese

version. I am always interested to see how different frames of

thought will approach the same matter, especially when this matter

is something as theoretically objective and universal as science.

Science is not supposed to be like art, where meaning and purpose

are largely a function of interpretation, though it is my inclination

that even science is somewhat of a gray area able to be subject to a

degree of interpretive bias. I purchased a ticket to the IMAX

theatre's tribute to Albert Einstein and the theory of relativity. I sat

and watched with my gigantic headset similar to the one I used to

drown the world out with in college as the show presented itself in

Chinese and I listened in English. It turned out to be a strange

phenomenon since I could hear the Chinese through my earphones

just as easily as I could hear the English emanating from the

speakers suctioned to my ears. I wondered about the possibility that

the same visual image of Einstein riding a lightning bolt into space

as part of a humorous demonstration of the minimal effect of time

in relation to an object traveling at the speed of light was possibly

being interpreted in profoundly different ways depending on which

language the audience heard the auditory portion of the show. Is

science the one common platform of thought where the eastern and

western worlds are on the exact same page? It is a gray area in my

opinion.

I returned to the water front and stared at the glowing

Hong Kong sky line before I headed back to the hotel and left for

Shanghai the next morning, this time with a proper visa. I emailed

Jamie from the business center at the airport hotel to notify him

about the likely possibility of missing a couple days of work due to

my unexpected detour. He didn't make a big deal about it when I

returned but the rest of Vision Asia was astounded by my story of deportation. Ironically most of the people I worked with had never in their entire lives as Chinese citizens ever seen Hong Kong and here I was a tourist in their eyes educating them about one of their own cities. Belinda told me it was nice to have "Mel Gibson" back in the office to keep her company. Maybe it was the wavy hair, or the classic American good looks but something about being compared to the likes of Mel Gibson did not exactly appeal to me, much as I doubt he would care to be measured against a Jew… unless that Jew be Jesus. And Jesus, Mr. Gibson is certainly not, for Jesus was no bigot. As a symbol of a young American adult in a foreign land without a meaningful understanding of American pop culture, I suppose Mel Gibson will do, much like Jackie Chan, for lack of a better term to stereotype all the Asians I went to high school with.

October 31st was my last day working at Vision Asia, as the focus of the remaining month and a half in Shanghai, China adjusted itself to partying and traveling, two crucial components of any recent college graduates' complete abroad experience. Ahmad and I met some very interesting characters during this period. We found ourselves rendezvousing at a lounge by the name of

Barbarossa situated exotically in the middle of a man-made lake in People's Square Park. A short bridge would guide across the moat and into the royal Moroccan themed tent where the heavy exhalation of smoke from the hookah tent caressed the gentle nighttime air with a tender and glowing defiance before its gradual and winding diffusion became bare to the human eye. Jonah, the bartender, a former Miami native, would mix us a couple strong blueberry mojitos, a new twist on an old Cuban favorite, on the house of course. Ahmad worked methodically like Oscar Schindler during which time his impressive talent for schmoozing and meeting new people lead us to all the perks inherent in being on a first name basis with many of the cities' club managers and bartenders. I was more laid back and not nearly as socially motivated in Shanghai, though I certainly appreciated Ahmad's abilities.

We met the "Italian Guys", Antonio and Armeno during a late night at Bar Rouge where Moet Chandon was the theme of the night. The Italian Guys were a couple of fashionable Italian playboys with their white jacket sport coats and their designer

Armani jeans. Coming from the United States I was not used to seeing heterosexual men so obsessed with style (outside of New York City at least), although eventually I came to realize that this is fairly typical of European males, especially those from Italy. Between the two, Armeno was the only Italian guy that could manage fluent English, having spent a couple years in his early childhood living in Chicago with his Native American Uncle. He would proudly suggest that he was more American than I am, which in a way I guess this is true, though he and Antonio both proudly represented Naples. I couldn't exactly manage to decipher exactly what their business in Shanghai revolved around. Something to do with importing and exporting mini-bike engines was the best I could gather. It was all the same to me anyway as they made an exciting and eclectic addition to our melting pot of international of acquaintances.

Katja, the German skydiver and ambitious young business lady with a thing for Chinese men (and women) was part of the abroad China program as well, and began to roll around with us to all the late night spots. Vision Asia was but a faded impression in my mind as I began to drown myself in the excess of the party scene once again. I drank because it made me feel the freedom of a lawless inner world of imagination and soul, a world I always willed for myself beyond the structure of parental and Jewish cultural expectations. My heart would thump with the beat of the Shanghai house music as the rapidly westernizing culture of thugged out Chinese "wanna be" gangsters would flow into the clubs like mindless drones struggling with the ancient traditions and the promise of the future. A brand new chrome plated ear piece rested decadently on the sides of their skulls to match their miniaturized $300 cell phone in one hand, and a cup of green tea with a dash of Jack Daniels Whisky to complement their other hand. In New Orleans we used to frequent a bar on the outskirts of a New Orleans ghetto called Butlers, a rundown shack complete with beefed up security guards, the best in gangster rap DJ's, an old school Atari in the corner, and the most eclectic collection of rich Tulane students and African Americans natives of the surrounding streets. The crowd would integrate with a distant harmony to it until a couple people finally got murdered and the bar was shut down. The Shanghai club scene in no way matched the intensity of the bar that was once Butlers no matter how hard the Chinese tried to

mimic the hip-hop culture of the West. It was a dilute replica at

best.

Eventually Ahmad and I decided it was time to take a trip

outside Shanghai, as his hot little Serbian girlfriend became the

source of more emotional annoyance than he was willing to deal

with, and similarly, Allie and I were in the mist of our own

relationship troubles as the distance between us was difficult for

both of us to bear. It was a solid month since she asked me to stay

with her in Prague and a lot has changed and neither of us had ever

handled being apart from one another with any type of emotional

maturity. Thailand was the destination and a mere four hours or so

away from the Shanghai Pudong Airport. We were all set to

purchase tickets until Ahmad remembered to check with the Thai

embassy website and see if his Lebanese passport would be enough

to get him across the border, which inevitably it was not as Thailand

exists as one of the many countries whose entrance requirements

are stricter with regards to Middle Eastern documentation. Ahmad

would have had to apply for a visa months in advance even though a US passport could pass through with ease. Considering my own recent experience with the Chinese immigration line, neither of us were willing to take a chance in Thailand and decided the island of Hainan, home of the famous beach town of Sanya the would be our destination.

We arrived at night after a two hour flight and immediately delighted in the instantly recognizable breeze of island wind. We took a taxi to Resort Horizon, situated beautifully atop the smooth ambiance of the Yalong Bay. The next morning we woke up and realized that aside from a Russian couple we had met the first night at the bar, Resort Horizon's vacationers were as homogeneously Chinese as Beijing's diplomatic cabinet. Gone was the mix of Americans and Europeans we were accustomed to in the metropolis of Shanghai. We realized quickly that we were in China's version of Florida, where the land of China comes to warm up and be a kid. Ahmad and I were sitting on the beach after an hour of dodging little light bulbed shaped jelly fish during our hour of snorkeling observing in astonishment as the Chinese vacationing men and women chased each other around the sand all wearing the same blue hotel robe in a game of what looked to us to be no more complex than "tag". They were like little children laughing and giggling as I postulated to Ahmad that only a country with a one child policy could produce such a childlike self indulgent "me" "me" attitude on display. It was like watching over a younger niece or nephew while they navigate the jungle gym at Chucky Cheese before spilling a soda on themselves and begging for more quarters to play the skee-ball.

Nevertheless, our time at Resort Horizon the first couple of days in Sanya were more than enjoyable. By the third day we decided to venture over to the Sheraton a few hotels down the beach to eat lunch and hopefully discover a finer crop of young ladies than what we found at the Resort Horizon. To our immediate surprise, within the first couple of minutes on the Sheraton property, we passed by some of the most beautiful women we had ever seen anywhere, let alone in China, let alone on the island of Hainan, the unexpected last place on the planet that either Ahmad or myself would ever dream to be the home of the Miss World Pageant '05. With the sped up impulsiveness found only in a true

ADD mindset like own, I reserved the rest of our stay at the Sheraton Hotel, which I rationalized was pennies a night cheaper than the Resort Horizon while boasting a much more attractive premises.

The second day at the Sheraton Ahmad received a call in our room from Miss Botswana's mother who was very worried about her daughter and tried vehemently with a thick African accent to reason with the Mandarin speaking front desk attendant to connect her to her daughter's room, the room of Miss. Botswana. The best the front desk could manage was our room, quite the arbitrary choice but nevertheless a blessing in disguise. Ahmad assured Miss Botswana's mother that we would find her daughter and have her call immediately. Ahmad and I immediately went downstairs and snuck past the prowl of the chaperones and over to a young beauty that turned out to be Miss France. We excused ourselves and asked her politely to direct us over to Miss Botswana as we had an urgent message from her mother. Miss France took this in a good humor and pointed across the hall over to Miss Nigeria and behind her Miss Botswana. Miss Botswana thanked us both with a sincere smile and whispered to me that Miss Nigeria has a crush on me. I laughed wondering if it was true, thinking it probably was and would not by a long shot represent one of the most outlandish propositions I have encountered. I told them to meet us later on at the bar and lounge in the lobby and to bring a handful of their friends. They agreed but never actually showed. I blame the chaperones.

I ended up spending the night with the pretty 20 year old Paraguayan vocalist who spent her days singing with a group of guitarists in order to serenade the hotel guests. Her voice was sweet and her hair was like a flowing stream of dark Wonka chocolate. We slept together and she spent the remaining hours of the night peeling the burnt layers of skin off my back as she repeatedly called me "serpiente", as she would apply more lotion to my rawly exposed skin. Ahmad still jokes that somewhere in China is a defiant Paraguayan boy with a Jewish nose and ADHD looking for his father.

A week later I was wandering aimlessly around Beijing with no sense of past or future …

Chapter 8: Homeless in Beijing

I purchased a round trip train ticket to Beijing soon after

Ahmad left for Miami. There was something about traveling to

Beijing alone that appealed to me, and I did exactly that. Shanghai's

train station was only two subway stops away from the Xin Yu In

and it was not overly difficult to navigate my way through the mass

of Chinese travelers and board my train. The ticket cost me fifty

American dollars, easily enough currency to feed a Chinese family

of 4 for a week and a half. I was the first of four members in my

sleeper cabin to arrive. One by one Shanghai's upper crust took

claim to their cot. The last to enter was a young man who's Tai Chi

like climbing ability lead him gracefully over my neighbor's cot and

onto the top bunk with the methodical artistry of a ballerina. The

atmosphere was friendly and non-committal as we all shared a

mutual respect for each other's space without any additional desire

to engage in even the most superficial of conversation. The young

lady next to me was dressed to compete among Shanghai's highest in societal stature. Sometime before I dozed off I recall having trouble dealing with whatever monstrosity of a fruit they decided to serve us along side our shredded pork and white rice. She explained to me robotically that this particular fruit is normally referred to as lychee, or the "dragon's eye". After peeling through the sharp outer membrane there was a lusciously moist inner fruit the size of a ping pong ball. It is actually quite sweet and tasty.

I fell asleep with ease as my body adjusted itself in anticipation of a long trip. I woke up intermittently to see the lights of one of many rather identical looking factory towns. The lights in our cabin turned on not long after the sun began to illuminate the sliding landscape outside my window. As we approached Beijing I remember seeing a handful of Chinese men and women in their backyards performing their morning Tai Chi sessions. I figure Tai Chi in the morning serves as a much healthier attempt at stimulating the senses in the morning than the rotten artificially induced caffeine jump that this country is so dependent on. As we pulled into the station I felt a reliable jolt of excitement that normally hits me when I have arrived at an undiscovered territory in my imagination. In preparation for my trip to Beijing all I had was a couple days worth of clean clothes and the address of the Holiday Inn I made reservations to stay in for the duration of my stay. It was early morning sometime in late November as the sole of my Nike Air made contact with the nearly frozen cement of the train station. I knew I had to act fast to find a taxi before the intolerable wind chill iced over my steady stride. Latitude wise Beijing resides about equal to the southernmost portion of Mongolia, which is nestled right below Russia.

Within minutes after emerging to the street my fingers began to move in slow motion due to the cold. I crossed to the other side of the street opposite the train station and hailed a cab about ten minutes later. With the best translation I could manage I spoke the name of the street of the Beijing Holiday Inn. The driver had no idea of the hotel's whereabouts and passed me on to another who knew of the street I was searching for. The hotel was just off a main highway running through the city and boasted a festively decorated marble floored lobby with an overexcited Christmas theme as a way to make all the western travelers feel at home. I approached the counter and spoke my name to the female clerk at the counter. She greeted me warmly and asked to see my passport. This question struck me as ludicrous. I explained to her that I traveled by train from Shanghai and that no passport was necessary for this particular means of transportation. She told me that all international travelers must show their passports when checking into a hotel in the PRC, (People's Republic of China). I subsequently assured her that I clearly was not an international traveler because I HAD ARRIVED FROM SHANGHAI, I was therefore a domestic traveler. At that point I was sure of two things: 1. I was right. 2. I was not going to win this battle.

The hotel clerk whose initial smile had morphed into an expressionless clinical void representative of the systematic red tape she was now guardian of told me coldly, "We cannot let you into Hotel without WISA" I said, "do you mean Visa" She said, "yes no entry without WISA". I walked away from the counter with the flooding realization that my trip to Beijing would have to be a very short one less I wanted to risk freezing to death on the streets. I walked for miles down the super highway that ran perpendicular to the street where the hotel domiciled looking for a crosswalk to get

across the street where I saw a China Construction Bank, one of the

bank's I knew would accept my ATM card. I thought to myself,

why in the world is there not even one opportunity to cross the

street? In New Jersey, the highway capital of the world, and the

state where I spent the majority of my twenty-three year old life in,

the cement highway divides have a gap in them approximately every

half mile to allow for a commuter to change direction with a U turn.

These same gaps provide brave pedestrians the opportunity to cross

over. I had never in all my experience seen a highway with no gap

in the cement divide until the day it was imperative that I cross the

street in the city of Beijing, China.

Finally I hailed a cab and told him to take me across the

street. He laughed and told me in indecipherable Chinese, "get out".

Of course he could have said anything to me and I would not have

known the difference but the message was loud and clear. Finally I

decided I would have to climb over the divide as the urgency of my

numbing fingers dictated. I made it through traffic and to the other

side with little conflict. From an aerial vantage point I must have looked like Frogger with my erratic movements in an effort to dodge an ever flowing stream of traffic. I believe this very concept is addressed in a Seinfeld episode where George has to carry an arcade sized video game machine across the street while maneuvering his way in between oncoming traffic.

I was able to withdrawal enough cash to pay for the 700 Yuan fare I would incur after a day with rogue taxi driver I had negotiated with prior to my trip to the bank. When I made it back to the Holiday Inn my driver was waiting in his early nineties Volkswagen Jetta, similar to the taxis in Shanghai except this one was jet black. I told the man at the door of the hotel that brokered our arrangement that I wanted to see the Great Wall of China followed by the Forbidden City. The Great Wall materialized within my consciousness about an hour outside the city of Beijing. At first glance, before I began to scale the immensely tiring set of stairs I felt a moment of Déjà vu. Just like in Shanghai and the rest of China, there were enough Chinese salesmen with their inane little gadgets, decorative tidbits, and homemade garments to entertain and clothe an island full of hyperactive toddlers. This time I bit though. It was imperative at that point, before I was going to climb another couple hundred of feet in altitude that I pay homage to my frostbitten fingers and numb skull with some mittens and a puffy red woven snow cap. Later when I communicated to my driver by raising two fingers with my right hand to indicate that I paid two American dollars for both items he told me I got ripped off.

I climbed the last of what seemed like an endless series of stone block steps whose height was chiseled out to be about a foot in height each. My lungs were so frigid I could feel them hardening and my organ systems slowing down. There were a couple tiers to the wall and at the top of each there were even more salesmen with more garments and more gizmos though the phenomenon was not nearly as plentiful at the bottom. My mind flashed back to an image of the men and women in American shopping malls with their mobile carts and personalized T-shirts and caps trying to make a buck. Funny how concepts are so universally connected and how your mind can make instantaneous connections to things worlds away faster than any of Pentium's most powerful and cutting edge processors. It is a certain fact that human life is becoming rapidly more dependent on machines as the economy continues to globalize but there is one thing a machine will never master in the foreseeable future, and that is abstract thinking. The day a computer develops the ability to think abstractly is the day machines are no longer confined to the actions in which they are programmed. It is also the day we run for our lives. Prophecy aside however, I have always had a real interest in the duality of the mind and the brain and what actually constitutes consciousness.

As I reached the pinnacle of my trip to the top step of the top tier on the Great Wall of China I looked out in sheer amazement as I watched the wall laterally snaking its way over around and in-between the hills for as far and beyond the horizon of my perception. I thought to myself at that very moment that all this trekking was going to be worth it in the long run, even though I have another hour ride back into the heart of Beijing to feast my eyes on the Forbidden City and I hadn't even given any thought as to how I was going to survive the night time in consideration of my WISA problem. In any case I took one last look at the grandeur of the Great Wall of China and climbed back down the stairs and back through the parking lot with the salesmen, tapped the window of the black Jetta to wake my trusty napping driver and we were off. I dozed off for a bit myself as we drove back toward the city though I did notice the sign on the highway to turn off for Ming's Tombs, the burial grounds of an ancient Chinese Emperor. Further past this point the mountainous vista in our rear view mirror gave way to a sprawling urban center with a crowd of little shops and Chinese men huddling around the warmth of their woks and steamers. I was dropped off about a mile outside the entrance to the Forbidden City as I traced the perimeter of the gigantic walls surrounding it. The Forbidden City from what I understand about Ancient Chinese History is that one can actually view it as a city within a city. The city outside the Forbidden City was poor and depressed while the city inside the walls represented all that is rich and decadent among the governing class and especially the Emperor himself. The peasants eventually became fed up with the aberrant inequalities and the Emperor was overthrown. In my eyes, it is another testament to the danger inherent in complacency and the failure to acknowledge those that are hungry and more competitive for food, money, intellectual progression, scientific innovation, or the very job one currently occupies.

The Forbidden City itself looked to me more like an expansive village rather than a city per se. It is quite a site no matter how you look at it though. Chinese tourists lined up from all over the land of China to breathe in the aroma of the bygones of an ancient civilization that was and is their own. You have seen sights from the Forbidden City in movies whether you realize it or not. There is a few hundred feet between the entrance and the Emperor's house for political gatherings and diplomatic rendezvous. As I navigated my way through the various houses and art galleries it more and more real to me. I found myself in the Emperor's garden and took a quick glance into a multitude of houses built solely for the Emperor's mistresses. Funny as it is to think about, or maybe not so funny depending on one's political association, each mistress was brought up to serve the King through years of training as part of a hierarchal institution. In other words there were different ranks or levels of mistress a female could occupy much like the various tiers to the Great Wall.

As the day went on and the cold long ago penetrated my brand new woven red hat and mittens I figured it was time to start really moving again as I drummed my way through the crowds and ultimately outside the walls of the Forbidden City. I exited from a different point than where I initially arrived in order to situate myself within a short distance of Tiananmen Square. The view of the square from across the street was dreamlike, almost as I had been there before. I took a stairway underground and surfaced minutes later. The wind blew alternately from every direction much like a racquet ball can blind side you from any angle. The flags in the air flew with greater affliction and prominence than the one that would sometimes send me into a trance on top of Bar Rouge over looking Pudong. After all, I was in the capital of Beijing, or Peking to the natives. It was a short and even eerie stay for me in Tiananmen; on one level the government buildings that enclosed the perimeter of the square reminded me of Washington DC with their noble stature and wisdom, though underneath the façade I could feel the suffering of the thousands of students and Red Cross workers who died in the 1989 massacre. Consistent with a long

tradition of the Chinese government's unwillingness to

acknowledge their own actions under the guise of censorship, a

Chinese resident can find himself in a heap of trouble if he were to

mention the massacre in front of the wrong government official.

Chinese tourists must keep their mouths shut as they gaze at one of

Beijing's greatest attractions while muting themselves

simultaneously. Tiananmen Square carried an odd medicinal feeling

to it, almost like the strange sensation one would feel when

breathing in the newly applied stench of bleach meant to cover the

mess of a blood soaked murder victim moments before your arrival.

After my self guided tour of Tiananmen I retraced my steps

back around the walls of the Forbidden City and over to the

parking lot that my driver was waiting in. Laughably he dropped me

back off at "my hotel" where he told me the price of his services

would be 800 Yuan, or about 90 dollars. Granted I was tired but I

remembered distinctly our negotiation called for 700 Yuan, not 800.

I chuckled at his foiled attempt and enjoyed a quick lunch at the

hotel buffet before I flagged another taxi and handed him the card with the Chinese characters meant to indicate train station. The sun was on its way down by this point in the day, after the solid seven or eight hours of my one day tour of China's capital city. While I would have liked to stay longer I did the best I could to condense my experience into the raw essentials of any westerner's touring expectations and I felt I did a fairly good job in light of the circumstances. I approached the ticketing window expecting to trade my one way ticket back, dated three days from that very moment, for a pass for that night. Unfortunately all the sleeper tickets were sold out and the only remaining vacancies were standing room only, a concept unheard of in the United States. I had two choices: 1. Stand shoulder to shoulder with other Chinese traveler's looking for the cheapest possible way to get to Shanghai for 11 hours on an overnight train or 2. Wander the streets of Beijing homeless, which in a sense I was already, and wait the three days out for my sleeper train.

Just as I was about to hand my money over to the attendant and purchase one standing room only ticket for what was roughly $10; I received an enthusiastic tap on the shoulder from an unidentified Chinese man. He was searching for recruits to fill his bus that was leaving for Shanghai within the hour. At first I was a bit hesitant about the proposition but considering the alternative I had to at least entertain the idea. He led me over to his bus almost entirely filled with eager Chinese travelers tucked neatly into their coffin sized personal sleepers. I handed the owner 30 Yuan, which ended up being cheaper than purchasing an entirely new sleeper pass on the train. Granted I would have stood the entire duration of the trip had I gone with the cheapest option but this to me seemed even more adventurous as I had a hard time even imagining a stretch of highway spanning the overwhelming distance between Beijing to Shanghai, over 1000 km to be more succinct. I boarded the bus and walked slowly toward the middle of the aisle before I threw my bag inside the basket at the end of the sleeper I would claim as my own on the top row. I jammed my feet inside the partially enclosed end of the "bed" and chuckled lightly at the scenario at hand. Picture yourself climbing inside a bobsled for the night with nothing but what seems to be raw cotton to keep you warm. As the bus departed one of the passengers approached me with the mischievous smile of a three year old and greeted me foolishly, "HELLO". Looking back it was the exact same hello my

friend Matt and I received in rapid succession from a long line of

little elementary school field trippers at the Shanghai museum of

Art.

Being I was the only English speaking passenger on a bus of

20 or so Chinese men the movie of choice, as expected, did not

have an English subtitles. Luckily it was still somewhat entertaining

to me with all the Kung Fu style martial arts exhibited. Often times

when I watch a movie my mind will tune out or fail to process

dialogue which has allowed me to focus in on and appreciate the

visual components of movies as an equally important aspect of the

film. Shortly after the first movie was finished we stopped off on

the highway about two hours outside Beijing and enjoyed a buffet

full of what I think, and very much hoped at the time was beef

alongside a never ending community bowl of white rice and other

random complements that escape my memory. I don't think some

of the people in the restaurant had ever seen a white man in their

entire lives as I received some pretty astonished glances as I did my

best to clamp down on my rice and beef specialty with my

chopsticks. There are certain aspects of etiquette that would catch a westerner off guard in China when first noticed. From what I have seen, a Chinese individual will not hesitate to stare at you for more than just a few moments if something captivates them. In the states it is of course rude to stare no matter how badly your eyes would like to lock onto the object or person of interest for just a few seconds longer. My friend and former co-worker Tiffany, who, as mentioned previously is about six feet and blond used to draw the most blatantly prolonged stares I have ever personally witnessed. While more and more Westerner's are flocking to China as I write this it is important to keep in mind that China is larger than the continental United States and there is still more area where the Chinese have not ever seen a white man or women than area where they have.

As the bus moved on I found myself dozing off midway into the second martial arts movie and ended up staying asleep for a solid four hours or so. When J woke up the bus was pitch black and silent as the only sounds that were audible to me was the whisk of the road flying by and the subtle sound of a man snoring in the back. The highway was dimly lit and I wondered for a second whether I was ever actually going to be back in Shanghai. I laid awake for the next couple hours in contemplation of my trip to Beijing and the somewhat ludicrous materialization of events. I fell asleep for a second time only to be awakened by the bus driver himself at around 7:00 am telling me that I had to get off and transfer to the next bus which happened to be parked parallel to our position. On top of his directions I could hear a chorus of "Hello, Hello, Hello" behind me as if to sing me off the premises. I smiled as I laced up my Nike Air's and boarded the next bus. The next bus was an ordinary blue colored bus like the last one except it boasted actual seats rather than little shelf like sleepers. I looked out the window for the next two hours as the landscape began to transition into the familiar light greenish brown marshland of outer Shanghai. We passed through Suzhou, a suburb of Shanghai oriented toward mostly rice fields, irrigation, and the occasional water buffalo. We made a couple more stops before we finally ended at the Shanghai Bus station near the outskirts of the French Concession and about a 15 minute taxi to the Xin Yu In.

By the time I returned from Beijing it was nearly December. I remained in Shanghai for about two weeks more. Ahmad had already been back in Miami and I wondered when, if ever, I would see him again. I spent my remaining days reading a lot and occasionally going out with the Italian guys, Katja, and even Angela tagged along on occasion. While I could probably write an entire book on my experiences in China alone I figure it is time to move on. I was back in Holmdel, NJ by mid December for what proved to be a painfully depressing wakeup call that it was time to figure out what was next, and fast. I had convinced myself, or at least partially convinced myself that the right thing to do coming back from Shanghai with no intention to go to law school or Medical school, that a Jew in finance would still make the family proud and allow me the chance to make a lot of money. It seemed to me that I was going to have to make a few adjustments, at least on the surface, to my once negative point of view toward the business world and especially corporate America. I knew philosophy was not going to pay the bills and I had my chance at medicine, and failed. My conversations with Allie were becoming more infrequent with passing time and that saddened me beyond measure as I knew we were slipping away from each other. I was going to have to suck this one up and get a job, and put the past behind me, despite the impossibility of that very notion.

Chapter 9: Morgan Stanley

Despite all I had gone through and the global expansion of my perspective on life, I was sucked back to NJ for the beginning of 2006 only to try and convince Morgan Stanley to hire a philosophy major fresh off the slow boat from China to sell mutual funds and alternative investments for them. It was going to be my last attempt at conforming for the love of my parents. After weeks of laying on the couch watching TV like a deadbeat lump of inanimate matter I knew the time to get a job, for the sake of my own sanity, would have to come sooner than later. Most of my friends were still in New Orleans, Miami, Shanghai, really anywhere outside of Holmdel. I had been communicating with my cousin Scott, an employee of the Merrill Lynch Investment Management division to prep myself for the various questions I would be confronted with as I interviewed for various entry level financial positions. Both my cousins, Steve and Scott have always treated me more like a little brother than a cousin and I have tremendous

gratitude for all the things they have showed me over the years.

When Scott heard I was interested in finance he did everything he

could to prepare me. We went over voice projection, basic financial

knowledge, potential interview questions and most importantly, my

mess of a resume. The entire idea of a resume in my mind was

completely unnecessary. Clearly one could not judge the true

content of one's character and to a large extent even their

intelligence by their grade point average and summer internships.

Scott told me about his giant stack of recommendations he

collected during his time in college and told me I should think

about emailing a couple of my professors to proposition that they

write me a couple as well. I figured this too was unnecessary as I

figured my own recommendation of myself upon interviewing

would suffice. I had never bothered to get to know any of my

professors in college anyway, and did not feel right asking them for

a recommendation despite the fact I was sure they would not have a

problem with any request of mine. It felt artificial.

There was one exception. Second semester senior year I had the same professor for my 200 level modern philosophy class and my 600 graduate level philosophy class, Empiricism. Oliver Sensen earned his PhD at Cambridge and spent a few years teaching at Harvard before electing to take a professorship at Tulane University. After he administered the second quiz of the semester he approached me after class and asked me why I was not performing at the high level he had come to expect at that point from my comments in class. He went on to tell me that I had a lot of potential and did not understand why my grades were not reflecting such. Almost four years at Tulane and this was the first I had ever heard such a thing from a teacher. I told him later on that I did not mean to insult him by failing to live up to my potential and that maybe my ADD had something to do with my underperformance. It was the first time I had ever used it as a scapegoat but I did not want him to lose his confidence in me, or re-think his comments from earlier in the semester. I could tell he took my comment seriously as if he really did believe that ADD could impede academic performance to an extent. Looking back I am sure he would have been curious to know most of the auditory components of his lecture never made it beyond the semi-permeable-membrane between the outside world and my brain.

In any case I did stop by and speak with him once after class. I cannot recall what the meeting was about but it was monumental in the sense that I voluntarily chose to meet with one of my professors beyond the class room setting. I think we discussed New Orleans college students' boozing habits but I couldn't say for sure. Later on when Katrina hit, which I only dodged by two weeks myself, I sent him an email to see if he and his family were okay. Allie accused me sucking up to get a letter of recommendation from him and I even admitted, falsely, that maybe it was the reason. It wasn't though. I genuinely cared that he made it out ok because to me there was no more valuable a professor on the Tulane Campus than Oliver Sensen. I never did ask him for a recommendation and resented the idea of asking any teacher even further after Allie's comment.

Back on sequence:

Scott looked at one of the last of my countless re- drafts and told me everything was spotless except that I would have a hard time convincing any employer that I was a professional snowboarder, as I boldly pointed out on my resume at the bottom under "activities". While I was a professional in my own mind he assured me that I would need to actually be sponsored or at least have a few medals in my possession to back my claim. I assured my cousin I would remove that element before any distributions were in order. My first interview was at Smith Barney for the financial consulting trainee program. Essentially this was a fancy name for a stock broker trainee program. I made it through the first interview and was invited back for a second. Luckily, my father's good friend Mark Smith was a financial advisor for the company I really wanted to work for, Morgan Stanley, and he was marvelous in his endeavor to secure me an interview with the Human Resources department of Morgan Stanley Investment Management, a division of Morgan Stanley much like the division my cousin Scott was employed at with Merrill Lynch. A job with MS Investment Management held a few key points of significance for me. For one I would not have to interrupt families during dinner with the latest in securities offerings

(though looking back it wouldn't have been so bad), and two, I

would be able to work with mutual funds, which I felt would be a

good segue into the hedge fund industry in due time. I went

through the first stage of interviewing with a lovely young woman

by the name of Jennifer Wolfe with flying colors, despite the fact

that I showed up on the wrong day and time.

Jennifer was in contact with the team at the Harbor Side

Financial Center in Jersey City to schedule the next round of

interviews. Carlo Aprea, Vice President and desk manager of the

Internal Sales Consultants greeted me warmly as I emerged from

the elevator and onto the third floor of plaza 2. He escorted me to

the interview room where I was to interview and ultimately present

a sales pitch on the topic of my choosing. We sat down face to face

and Carlo asked me in his own self-amused manner, "So,

professional snowboarder, huh?" I belted out a chain of curses a

mile long inside my head while outwardly maintaining my

composure with a slight chuckle while politely informing him that

he must have been given an outdated resume. I reached inside my black leather folder and handed him my most recent copy since Scott's latest array of constructive criticism. Imagine my relief when Carlo transitioned into his own miniature monologue as he told me about the new Burton snowboard he just received for Christmas and the house he rents with a few of his friends in Vermont. It is funny how things tend to work in my favor based on some of the most random of circumstances. It was at that moment that I thanked Mrs. C inside my mind for convincing me to use snowboarding as my topic of choice for my sales pitch rather than The Simpson's, my favorite TV show.

Mrs. C explained to me a couple days before my interview my topic needed to come from the heart and represent something that projects the image of a "go getter" and a "doer", rather than one who merely sits on the couch and takes pleasure in a television show. I agreed and found that I didn't even need the two index cards of bullet points I had prepared the night before. I pictured myself on the mountain in my usual HD quality imagery and manufactured in my mind the tranquility of the mountains and the continuity of thought and action I would delight in as I surf the snow. My body language was in sync with my thoughts, and my speech, which has the tendency to stall itself on occasion like a motor boat running on fumes, was just as fluid. It's truly wondrous how easily I could execute a simple sales pitch on why I enjoy snowboarding and why others might like it as well. When spoken from the heart words have a magical way of being there when you need them. The remainder of the interview following my presentation went extremely well as the two members of the team Carlo chose to sit in on the presentation took a noticeable liking to me. Two agonizingly long weeks later Jennifer Wolfe called me with an offer of employment from Morgan Stanley to be an Internal Sales Consultant for the mutual fund desk.

My first day of work was February 6th, 2006. I would wake up around 6:30 and take the 7:20am train into Newark Penn Station where I could transfer to the Path train into Jersey City. Overall the commute took around an hour. Carlo checked me in the first day since I hadn't received an official ID for entrance. I was introduced to everyone and kept to myself at my seat for the first couple of weeks taking in the new atmosphere and learning as much about the products I was to sell as soon as Carlo gave me the okay to "go live" on the phones. Admittedly, I was anxious well into the first few months at Morgan. Carlo would call me into his oversized cube every other day to check in on my progress and train me. I was clearly uncomfortable with one on one conversation and found myself fidgeting as Carlo would lecture me on various financial concepts. I found myself staring blankly back at him sometimes as he asked me simple questions, questions whose answer I certainly knew but the knowledge was of little help to me since I did not know what he was asking me. I was still about 10 months away from realizing that I have trouble hearing what is being said to me, and that entire conversations can expire without my processing a word of it, at least on a conscious level. I would leave Carlo's cube even more anxious and upset than when I would enter it because I knew Carlo was beginning to wonder about me.

Working in the Corporate World forced me to face many things about myself because it is a closed and even somewhat controlled environment where repetitive behaviors tend to magnify themselves in conjunction with a constant setting. In school I could always bounce around from place to place, class to class. In the corporate world I was forced to sit at the same desk for at least eight hours and interact with the same people. I hadn't let anyone this close to me in years and all the sudden I found myself thinking about such things as relationship management. There was no opportunity to hide behind the chaos of my scattered life and scattered brain as the workday called for at least eight hours a day, Monday through Friday, of exposure to the same place at the same time with the same people. They were a good group of individuals though, and all characters in their own right. I adapted relatively quickly and earned the reputation early on as the type of person to push the limits on things. Greg McCabe and I were notoriously known as the two rookies who brazenly placed one order each of Johnnie Walker Blue on the company tab at the Havana Club amongst the likes of Al Sharpton and Alec Baldwin in Mid-town Manhattan our third and second weeks on the job respectively. Later on when others were talking about what had been done, I over heard someone say that, "B-Rob did it".

B-Rob caught like wild fire throughout the following couple of months as my behavior became increasingly fearless and somewhat outlandish. March was my first month on the phones and I was number one in activity points (points allotted based upon number of outbound, inbound, and left messages to financial advisors regarding MS funds), virtually every day. Since training had ended I was no longer subjected to regular one on one lectures from Carlo and he was able to focus more on my hunger to prove myself on the phones and my charismatic way with some of the advisors when I engaged them. I found that as long as my vision was locked on some sort of object in motion, whether it be a person across the room, or a boat floating past my beautiful view of the Hudson River, or a helicopter in the sky patrolling the NYC skyline, I was able to pay attention to what was being said to me on the phones with greater clarity and act accordingly. It wasn't perfect but it helped. As time went on I began to get more proficient with the products and the industry. In early May Carlo dropped a four inch thick binder on my desk labeled Securities Training Corporation. It was the Series Seven manual. For those not familiar with finance, the Series Seven legally allows for an individual to sell securities such as stocks, bonds, mutual funds, funds of hedge funds, and so forth. Each internal was given three chances to pass the test, and just so happened the employee MS brought me into replace had been transferred to another department after failing at all three attempts. I knew I could not take any chances. I went home that day and asked my dad for a prescription for Adderall 10mg to take in the evening to help me focus.

Ryan Kulik, the newest internal to join since I came on board was promoted from the customer service desk and had already taken a look at the Series Seven material. We were scheduled to attend series seven classes at the Double Tree Hotel in Manhattan for the month of May twice a week after work. Inevitably Ryan began attending class by his lonesome as the class was not doing me any good, as usual. My self made curriculum would consist of one-hundred-percent self study with the help of my little blue pills, or vitamin A, as the kids sometimes call it these days. At first one was enough to give me the neuro-stimulative high that my brain would crave in the pursuit of page after page of the laws and regulations put forth by the SEC. While there was some good in learning the Series Seven material, for instance my knowledge base was growing and my confidence inflating as I spoke more fluently to advisors on the phone, the fact was I needed the Adderall to sit me down in one place and study for more than ten minutes at a time. Soon two or three Adderall a day transformed into a mandatory four to get me going on the mundane material that was 85% of the series seven material. Even with the artificial enhancement to my attention span that Adderall would induce in me, I still found myself zoning out into Bri Bri land, the only difference was I had a better time sitting in one spot as my impulsiveness to move around and fidget had been minimized.

I took the Series Seven in early July and passed with an 80%. Ryan received an 88%. With seventy as the minimum passing grade I was proud of myself for exceeding the minimum by 10 points, and I was proud of Ryan for his score as well. By this time in my life I had learned to taper my expectations as far as high scores on tests were concerned. I graduated Tulane University with a 2.3 grade point average which was enough to earn me a diploma, and in my mind, a seventy would have been enough for me to be happy with the mere fact that I passed the Series Seven. The extra ten points were icing on the cake as far as I was concerned and Ryan beating me by 8 points did not irritate me the least bit. Adderrall was my secret weapon at that point and despite the anti-social effects it had on me, I figured if I designated the drug consumption to an as needed basis, I could pass any test with evening study and still go to work, where I was expected to be at least somewhat social and salesman like, unmedicated.

By August I had passed the Series 66, which is the combination state law and portfolio management examination. Most internals let at least a year go by before tackling the 66 and with the help of Adderall I was able to pass it with only three weeks preparation, granted with a 72%, but never the less people were shocked with the two accomplishments spaced together so closely. I found myself meriting more respect in the work place as my co-workers' perception of me became less that of a punk kid fresh out of college and more of an ambitious young "go getter". Of course the B-rob persona was at its peak as I found myself cracking the whole desk up with some of my outlandish tell it like it is comments. Clearly I had a problem with authority in their eyes as I would not hesitate to argue my point of view with any individual in upper management. Unfortunately, the more I learned about the financial services industry, the more I became disillusioned by it. The corporate world was too systematized and political for a free thinker like me to ever truly be happy. I struggled to find meaning in the work I was doing and found very little to work with. I loved the people I was with and that kept me going for a while but predictably it was not enough to sustain my spirit. I once again turned to adderall in September to study for my Chartered Financial Analyst designation. I decided that I would have to get out of sales since I was having more and more trouble being salesman like, or as I saw it, phony in my endeavor to represent products I didn't necessarily believe in.

My ACT score began to drop off steadily as my relationship between the external wholesaler I was assigned to began to take on its share of stress as well. It was my job to support his efforts out in the field as he would speak to the same advisors in a face to face setting that I was busy calling upon from Jersey City. Our territory consisted of Southern California, including Los Angeles in addition to the Las Vegas area in Nevada. Andrew was in a sense my boss just as Carlo was and it was my job to follow up with any advisors he may have met with recently in addition to fulfilling the various merchandise orders he would allot to the advisors to encourage them to keep doing business with Morgan Stanley Funds. I would end up receiving these orders and ultimately botching them. On top of that, the various administrative tasks he would ask me to do would often times remain unfinished as I told myself I was too focused on my own independently drawn up call campaigns to focus on Andrews orders. Looking back that is only half the truth. My desk was always a cluttered mess and the notes I took for myself to remind myself of some of Andrew's directions were indecipherable to even my own two eyes. I could not read my own writing and found myself zoning out even worse than usual as Andrew gave me directions. Meanwhile Carlo was perfectly happy with the quality of phone calls I was making but Andrew on the other hand was getting fed up with what he perceived as laziness and lack of follow through on my part.

I could tell by Andrew's voice that he did not feel entirely comfortable in reprimanding me over things such as untimely submission of merchandise orders or lack of perseverance in scheduling appointments with big business advisors but he managed. Meanwhile as a coping mechanism I told myself that I was not threatened by his or anyone else's higher position or status and it was up to me, as it always has been, to distinguish between authority I respected and that which I did not respect and henceforth would not comply with. Again, this is only half the truth. There were times where I would truly give it my all to fulfill all the merchandise orders and make all the appointments and I still couldn't get my act together. In school I thought I was too cool, at work I convinced myself I was too righteous, but in the end there was still a certain antagonizing perfectionism that I demanded from myself. While I did not believe in what I was doing completely and my psyche was wilting from the perceived meaninglessness of my endeavors, I remained very upset with myself because I did not want to let anyone down, including Andrew. It was time to begin taking Adderall in the daytime. I scheduled an appointment with Dr. Van Hove, my childhood psychiatrist, the same doctor who diagnosed me as ADHD at seven years of age. She gladly wrote me a script for 25 mg of adderall XR (time released) and another script for 10mg instant adderrall for studying in the evening.

The first week of September represented my first week back on Adderrall during the daytime since junior year of college and it had a noticeable anti-social effect on my personality. While certainly medication can yield different effects when combined with the unique chemical makeup of each individual's brain, I found for myself that the medication quashes a certain charisma inherent in my nature. I knew this to be the case but I rationalized that sacrifice was part of life and part of growing up was giving a little to get a little. Adderall helped my mind to calm down and focus on the same task and did wonders for my merchandise fulfillment success ratio. I told Andrew that I was taking Adderall to assist my efforts in some of the administrative tasks I had proved to be unreliable with in the past. He understood, and admitted that he even took a drug called Straterra to help him with his own mild case of ADD. The more he got to know me the more he began to recognize my deficits and utilize my strengths. It meant a lot to me as the months

went on and the tone in his voice began to sing the music respect.
It made me want to work harder for him even if it did take me
twenty minutes to complete one merchandise order when it took
other internals no more than five. The Adderall helped me to
endure the extra fifteen minutes necessary to complete the orders.
Unfortunately it didn't stop with the merchandise. I was bombarded
by 20-30 emails a day consisting of either directions from Carlo or
Andrew, orders or fund inquiries from advisors, marketing
procedures and protocol from compliance, and so forth. All of
which proved to be more than my scattered mind could handle. I
made the decision sometime in mid September that I would have to
earn my CFA level 1 (normally requires a year's study) in three
months in order to be promoted by early 2007. I needed a secretary
to handle my administrative duties so that I could concentrate on
the conceptual side of the business. I knew I would thrive in a
setting where I could wrestle with concepts and theory all day, and
the CFA was my means to get there, and Adderall my ticket.

Chapter 10: Addiction

By late July, following my bump in salary and right to earn

commissions since passing the Series 7, I had moved out of my

house and into a studio in downtown Manhattan just a few blocks

from Union Square. I chose to live alone despite two different

offers to room with a couple of my friends. There is something to

say, at least to me, about reining sovereign over your own territory,

and I needed solitude in order to focus on my studies. By

September I was taking 25 mg of Adderall in the daytime and a few

at night to keep focused and in one stationary position for hours at

a time. It was getting urgent, at least in my own mind, that I pass

CFA level 1 and move up the corporate ladder and find the

intellectual stimulation and meaning in my work that I needed.

Aside from that, I had rationalized that I needed to be in a position

where I could have a secretary to help me with my administrative

follies. Looking back these were some pretty lofty short term goals

I had set for myself to accomplish. The way I saw it, being a Jewish individual in the shadow of his successful father, if I wasn't chairman of the World Bank by 27, or somewhere comparable, then I would be a failure. The fact was, however, I was not happy, and the Adderall had the ability to tranquilize my feelings about my perceived lack of meaning in finance and to concentrate on the logic of what it would take to advance and mold myself into the ideal of success and wealth.

My life had become fully consumed with the sole purpose of passing the CFA level 1 in three months time as I cut off all social contacts and even my own family to an extent. The drugs were taking over as I was able to manipulate it so that Dr. Van Hove would write me one prescription for Adderall and my dad would write me another. Before long, my mind was swimming and wadding in the artificial pool of insanity that Adderall had eventually shaped for me. Some nights, I would spend the whole night studying and go to work with zero sleep. My co-workers and my boss did begin to notice the change in me as I became increasingly less participatory in the joking banter I was known to include myself in before I began studying for the CFA. Two things were happening to me: 1. I was stressing myself out with the CFA, and 2. I was falling deeper into what ultimately turned into a severe problem with Adderall addiction. Luckily, my co-workers and Carlo attributed the perceived change in me only to number 1 since the CFA is known to be the most grueling exam in finance with a less than 40% pass rate, and this allowed for problem number 2 to slip under the radar. Before I go any further I take full responsibility for the Adderall abuse I subjected myself to during those three months of disaster. I was dishonest with both Dr. Van Hove and my father when requesting a new script for the drug, as I would often times fail to mention to one that I had seen the other and already received a new dose.

On average I was getting 2-3 hours of sleep a night Sunday through Friday, while crashing for approximately 10 hours on Saturday. I began to lose weight as my appetite had been severely diminished from the adderall abuse. I was even beginning to lose some hair. There were many nights where I didn't bother to have dinner at all, as long as my body received a healthy serving of 30 to 40 mg of instant adderall on top of the time released capsule I took in the mornings. Food was not a luxury I could afford myself with the CFA coming up in December and precious little time to waste on anything besides studying. It was imperative that I accomplish the impossible, I told myself, and the only way to do this was by living a less than healthy existence, if only for the next few months. My world grew more insane by the day as my eyes began to develop little red veins around the periphery and the skin below my bottom row of eyelashes began to droop into themselves. My mind was literally restless even as my body was sleeping. Sleep paralysis was not an unfamiliar phenomenon to me. As far back as I can remember I would occasionally find my body paralyzed as if I am stuck inside a coffin while my mind perceives with full awareness. It was of the few things that would actually scare me, though I would always inevitably fall back asleep. With the adderall I found myself in a dream world of sleep paralysis, never fully knowing if I was awake or asleep.

I would go to my financial accounting class in mid October convinced that I was being followed. I would sit in a manic haze as my teacher went over assets, liabilities, and so forth, all the necessary prerequisite knowledge for the CFA exam. I was absorbing nothing and convinced myself that I needed even more Adderall so that I could focus. I never could focus inside any classroom but Adderall was supposed to work. My instants would run out in a little more than a week's time since I was taking at least 4 times the normal dose on a nightly basis. I began to take the time release Adderralls in place of them. The consequences of this decision further contributed to my pre-existing state of delirium since the time release Adderall would last anywhere between 8-12 hours unlike the instants which wouldn't last past 5 hours. By November I was a malnourished insomniac yet I still managed to go through the motions of work during the daytime. I even found an article on Real Estate Investment Trusts in the Economist that highlighted the case for purchasing into a couple of our real estate funds that ended up turning into a national marketing campaign for Morgan Stanley Investment Management. Looking back I do not fully understand how I made it through work each day and studied all night for three months straight. Granted my ACT numbers began to drop with each passing month but, again, I was studying for my CFA so it was not seen as a big deal.

In late November I decided that I would meet with a girl

my parents had set me up with for brunch in Red bank, NJ. I am

normally very hesitant to partake in anything of that nature if my

parents have something to do with it, but it was different this time.

I remembered this girl from my days at Ranney. It was Jessica Welt,

the girl who used to let me climb in her locker and subsequently

shut the door on me. Mind you by late November I was in no shape

to charm women after more than two months of heavy

amphetamine abuse. We met for breakfast and spoke about various

topics of which I cannot recall. I paid for breakfast and we went our

separate ways as I needed to catch a train back to New York in

order to get back in time to get a full day of studying. Our meeting

felt like a dream and my recollection of it was foggy and surreal, but

my subconscious did pick up on one thing that played back like a

quick time video clip in my mind: "YOU ARE A VISUAL

THINKER". Why was this point such an important revelation, I

thought to myself sitting back on the train, especially since I simply

shrugged the idea off as nothing at the time? I did some research

and found that visual spatial thinkers are commonly right brain oriented and often times share a co-morbidity with those, like myself, who have been diagnosed with ADD. I discovered a website by Linda Silverman PhD, one of the leading pioneers in special education with a focus on the visual thinker and the gifted visual thinker. The idea that excited every nerve of my body however, was the concept of the combination learning disabled gifted visual thinker, otherwise known as a twice exceptional learner, or as she calls them, "Lost Treasures."

According to Linda's research, I found that the learning disabled, gifted visual thinkers, the "2E" (twice exceptional) learners are at high risk in childhood, especially if their learning disability remains undiagnosed. For one, with their distinct intellectual abilities, they are able to abstract around their learning disability to the point where the educational system may simply view them as average or above average at best in terms of academic performance and intelligence. In other words their giftedness (or sometimes creative genius) is muted by their learning disabilities and their learning disabilities are never diagnosed due to their counteracting giftedness. The two forces balance each other out and the school fails to recognize their amazing capabilities and in turn the student fails to recognize their own capabilities without the positive reinforcement of a system designed for a very different type of thinker and learner. Through Linda Silverman's research, she was able to discern that there is a high incidence of auditory processing or auditory inattention problems coupled with gifted visual thinkers and this is what manifested the idea of this particular type of twice exceptional learner in the first place. Often times these children exhibit symptoms of ADD/ADHD due partly to the obvious fact that if a student is not "hearing" what is being said in class, it is logical that one would be more inclined to fidget and day dream while the rest of the class is actually learning.

I distinctly remember the day I was sitting in my seat and talking to my friend Mike Marulli, who sat next to me, and coincidentally graduated Holmdel High School right before I entered as a freshman, and another friend of mine, Pryha, who I also shared a great working relationship with. Pryah began asking me questions about the CFA and my mind was creating some sort of hallucinogenic effect (Adderall induced, I am sure), almost as if

160

to tell me something. Pryah's mouth was moving but there was an odd cloudlike visual blocking the sound coming from her mouth. It looked similar to the censors you might see in front of the mouth of a television character using profanity, but with a hazier and more surreal like property to it. With all the pain and suffering I was putting my brain through at the time; it was evident to me that my subconscious was trying to tell me something. I WAS NOT HEARING A WORD SHE WAS SAYING. It occurred to me later that night, even on the drugs that perhaps this is something I have always had. As I did more research in addition to what I had already figured out about visual thinkers in the class room, I found that auditory processing disorders, coupled with thinking in pictures is also commonly found in autism. I began to wonder if my sense of feeling different and outside of things was attributable to the world of an autistic.

As I fell deeper into addiction and with the test less than a week away there were days where my Adderall intake exceeded 100mg as one day would speed into the next. I was sacrificing everything for this exam, my friends, my sleep, my sanity. I found myself crying for no reason. Luckily, when the situation was at its very worst I was able to conceal it from the work place since they had granted me the last week off before the exam to study. I would lay in my apartment with no sense of time or appetite while my mind began to hallucinate. I closed my eyes at one point and there was Jesus inside my mind, illuminated brilliantly with the intense coloration and the full multi- dimensional lucidity of my mind. As I remember it, he was placing some sort of crown atop his head. It was a true master piece as far as psychotic visualizations go… I'm Jesus! I am convinced. I feel this rush of euphoria like an orgasm throughout my entire body.

I am Jesus, I keep telling myself!

Later on that week I was walking back from Chipotle, one of the few times I had actually convinced myself that it would be a good idea to nourish myself, when a beam of yellow light shot out horizontally in the face of my vision field and literally caused me to lurch back in an attempt to dodge what struck me as a strange laser beam of energy. I told myself it had to be the drugs, and chuckled to myself as my heart was beating like a drum.

By the time I arrived at Jacob Javits Center on the west side of Manhattan for the sitting of the CFA level one exam I was doomed. I hadn't slept in two days and my mind and body were in desperately fragile form. I lost ten minutes from the very beginning after carelessly removing the wrong calculator from my backpack. My head was struggling to even read the questions let alone think and calculate. It was an absolute disaster looking back; though the drugs kept my hope alive with the time released euphoria that Adderall can be counted upon for. Following the exam I found it harder and harder to get through the day at work. The CFA results were not to be announced for at least a month and I still had a problem that needed addressing. My parents had finally seen enough change in me that they referred me to a psychiatrist in New York and I went under my own will as I knew I had a problem that needed to be dealt with. I admitted to Dr. Jacobs as soon as we sat down together that I had a problem with Adderall. I disclosed to him that there were times where I had consumed over 100mg on a given day and I hadn't slept like a normal human being since September. I even opted not to go out for New Years despite numerous invitations to attend various parties.

Dr. Jacobs appreciated my candor and of course recognized immediately that there were some ADD like issues that I struggled with including possible learning disabilities, as he called them, which needed additional exploration. I had never thought of myself as learning disabled until recently. In fact, I almost resented the term after seeing my sister sent to a boarding school for the learning disabled, a term that resonated to me as nothing more than a home for the children of rich lazy parents who do not feel like putting forth the effort to raise their own children. I soon learned that LD is a real phenomenon and can have serious consequences for the children afflicted and their parents. Dr. Jacobs knew that despite my problem with Adderrall, it was still the best medication for those individuals like myself with ADD and ADD like symptoms and he gave me one more shot at taking the pills responsibly and wrote me a new prescription. I told Dr. Jacobs that the Adderall was no longer a problem and my ability to take them under the prescribed dosage, 25mg a day and ten at night as needed for studying, would not be under question. Interestingly enough, I had never struggled with any type of addiction in my life and even my experience with Adderall addiction, in my opinion, was not a chemical dependency, but rather a product of the circumstantial context of my life, a context that had not changed even after the CFA exam as little else had really changed.

My second episode of Adderall induced psychosis took place in the third week of January, '07. I could not resist taking 2 or 3 instant adderralls instead of one per night. I would come home from work and lay down on the futon in my studio lonely and not fully content with the life I was living. I had shut friends out of my life since, and even before my problem with Adderrall and something just wasn't right. I had to keep myself occupied and decided to do some research on a book I had been planning on writing about learning disabilities, ADD, and so forth. On the research end, I felt the instant Adderall would give me the boost I needed to stay focused on my endeavor, and quadrupling my prescribed dose would provide me with an even larger boost. I found myself one night dealing irrationally with the numerical digits of my birth date and before I knew it I was reading page 620 (I was born on 6/20/83) of the Orthodox Jewish Bible, a bizarre choice considering my history. I called my Dad, which looking back was probably a subconscious cry for help, and told him that I was ready to fulfill my duties as the messiah, as dictated on page 620 of the orthodox Jewish Bible. My father knew there was something very wrong about the situation and cancelled his entire day of patients to drive up with my mother and check on me.

When they arrived I had already planned my first undertaking as the new messiah. I proposed to my parents who sat across the room from me on the floor of the kitchen in my apartment that either George Bush withdraws the troops from Iraq, or he would have to watch as a young American dies of hunger in front of his own eyes. There I was a couple hours into my hunger strike in defiance of an issue that I had not been particularly vocal about prior to my demonstration. After four hours my father called the paramedics and even recommended that they bring a few NYPD officers with them, as he knows how fast and strong I can be both physically and mentally when in opposition to something I believe in. While the whole display was artificially induced by the drugs, and it was true that I did not feel nearly as strongly about the issue of war in Iraq, I feel my father's decision to include a couple of New York's finest was probably the right decision. My mother watched over me as I heard the sound of a radio and the hustle of footsteps climbing the stairs like someone had lost track of a herd of buffalo. It took about a fourth of a millisecond just by the sound for me to figure out what was happening as I quickly retreated to my cozy loft overlooking the rest of my studio, the very loft I used to sleep on and wake up with lumps on my head each morning as a result of the foot and a half of negative space between my nose lying horizontally, and the ceiling above. I knew I could buy myself some time up there since most cops on average, would not be expected to be able to fit up there with me with all the doughnuts they eat.

I knew from their faces when they finally did enter the room that they were reasonable men and were not looking to incarcerate me, but rather to help me. I told them right away that the last thing I wanted to do was get in a physical showdown with a couple of New York City Police officers but they had no right to barge in and escort me out of the very apartment that I pay for myself with the money that I earn. I was not hurting anyone, though as I understand from my studies in political philosophy class, society has the right to intervene not only when an individual is a threat to others, but also when an individual is a threat to himself. While I did not view it as such at the time, looking back I certainly was a threat to myself, and my parents, with the assistance of the police and the paramedics, did the right thing. I had the option of cooperating and climbing down from the loft under my own free will or being carried off against my will. While a younger adolescent me barely ever backed down from a fight, the last thing I wanted, even in a state of psychosis, was to hit a policeman for obvious reasons, but most importantly because they did not deserve to be hit. My solution was to come down and as a statement of passive non-compliance, have them cuff me before they walked me out.

Both my parents were visibly upset by the time I arrived at St. Vincent's emergency room not more than two blocks from my apartment on 12th street and Seventh Avenue. The paramedics and I were engaged in friendly conversation on my way over about high school wresting after they noticed the blue Holmdel Wrestling Hoodie I had chosen to wear over. When I climbed out of the ambulance they had already removed my cuffs since I was no longer a threat in their eyes. I was pretty cocky about the whole ordeal for awhile until the drugs finally began to wear off. I told the attending psychiatric resident that truly I was not mentally ill and if she would just wait for the drugs to wear off she would be able to see that with her own eyes. As the hours ticked past, I was beginning to get impatient and even worried that they were going to admit me with some sort of mental disease rather than let me loose. I found out later that one of the diagnoses they were working on before the drug test came back positive was Schizophrenia, one disorder I knew for a fact I did not have, despite the occasional eccentricities I have been known to exhibit from time to time. Luckily I began to come out of it in the nick of time and did not fit the criterion for an overnight stay, though I was given the option to stay if I chose. My parents drove me home not long after I was given the "okay" to leave. The doctor's prognosis was simple: Catch up on my sleep, feed my malnourished body, and never touch Adderall again!

It is not a surprise to me that the country of Canada has already banned Adderall nationwide. The drug, while helpful in some respects is extremely addictive and excessively abused by college students and the like and has even been known to cause arrhythmia and sudden death in rare cases. I am lucky to be alive after what I went through with the drug and would encourage the parents of any children on Adderall to monitor their children closely should a doctor prescribe it to them to treat the symptoms of ADD/ADHD or any other "developmental disorders" or "learning disabilities". It is my own prognosis that we ought to focus more on what makes these individuals different and unique rather than medicate them to make them more like everybody else. The cases of ADD/ ADHD and related disorders have multiplied significantly even since I was diagnosed around the age of seven. Is it fair to call it an epidemic, or is society finally willing to accept that what we may really be looking at here is an innovative breed of thinkers coupled with a certain element of incompatibility with the current system. Many of the ADD/ADHD and LD individuals I have come across in my twenty-three plus years of life exhibit incredible bursts of charisma, creativity, and accomplishment, and I for one do not wish to suppress any of the gifts inherent in my own abilities for the sake of an increased ability to focus on things that I frankly do not have any interest in pursuing in the first place. The largest contributor to my problem with Adderall, as I mentioned before, was not chemical by any means, but instead, spawned from the hard realization that without the artificial impetus that Adderrall could provide, I was unable to go through the motions of a life I did not want for myself, despite the apparent positives of my existence. That day, while imprisoned for hours inside St. Vincent's I had made the decision to leave finance and Morgan Stanley.

Chapter 11: Coast to Coast

After much reflection one thing was all too apparent: I was once again jobless and trapped inside my parent's home. I felt like a caged lion that had just rediscovered his roar. All that I had been through had been so surreal and dream like, as I suppose even the present possesses such a quality through my eyes. The house itself is beautiful, really a monument to my father's hard work and dedication to becoming the successful surgeon that he is. A Jewish mother's pride and joy, my father is. He had never been arrested like his son, never struggled academically. Part of me had always wanted to escape the expectations inherent in being a Jewish young man. I had burnt through all my options and the harder I tried to fit the mold, a mold I had resisted in waves all of my life, the further I deviated from this ridiculous ideal. How in the world was I going to make an upper six figure salary sitting at home having resigned from my job at Morgan Stanley, my last shot at the big money?

I had always been rebellious so why was this bothering me so much in the first place. If I wanted to be this cookie cutter well behaved robot of a person I suppose I could have made that choice, and to be honest, the only way to battle nature, as man has figured is through technology. Adderall was technology for my brain, but experience has taught us time and time again that man cannot conquer nature, but can only hope to contain it. Since moving back to my house from New York City I felt like a child, not fully registering what I had been though, and impulsively chose to give the Doctor gig one last try, being that I only had two classes left to qualify for Med School, a foreign one that is, I signed up for Chemistry Two. I rationalized that of the three options every good Jewish boy has to make it big, being a Doctor still represented the most altruistic of them all, and it would not be hard to derive meaning from such work, while of course providing me with the opportunity to make a lot of money.

Somehow I convinced my NY psychiatrist to prescribe me Ritalin, another stimulant used to treat ADHD type symptoms. A couple weeks through chemistry at Community College and I was at least passing, but I knew at some level that I had truly thrown myself into the same unhealthy cycle of thinking that I had been struggling with for years. It did not take long for me to begin abusing the Ritalin. I would lock myself in my room and stare blankly at the Chemistry text. I had taken Organic already, but had failed Chemistry 2 at Tulane, the supposed pre-requisite to Organic. Oh well. In any case my mind was speeding and the only truly interesting concept I took to heart was that of entropy, which in my mind equaled out to this idea of increasing universal chaos, of which my wandering soul could relate. Chaos, interconnected universal forces, maybe G-d, call it what you will. I was so high on Ritalin one day that I found myself crying as I walked out of class, knowing that the way things were going, I was never going to be a Doctor, while simultaneously wondering if Jesus really had visited me that day in my Manhattan apartment just before my hospitalization.

I came home to my mother, eyes dry at that point, and luckily, as perceptive as she is, she had no idea I was nearing another breaking point. She told me that Harold Sylvester had left a message that he wanted to speak to me in regards to a show based upon a portion of a book I had written. This is of course in reference to the book you are reading right now. As a background for this, Harold is a Tulane alumnus and Emmy award winning actor and writer. I knew him as Griff from Married with Children and figured it would be a long shot, but possibly he would take a look at an unfinished version of this book, not even really thinking what could possibly be done with it. He was gracious enough, being a member of the Tulane Alumni directory to agree to read what I had written. A month went by and I had forgotten that he had a copy until my mother explained to me with enthusiasm and pride that he had just flown back from Europe and wanted to speak to me that night.

I called him that night at 8:00pm and the first words out of his mouth, having just read through my writing in raw form, were, "Brian Hey man let me tell you"…I waited with eager anticipation, "You are one piece of work", to which I responded, "Yeah, well, I get that a lot". We talked from there about creating characters for a show based upon my view of the world and specifically my two

Tulane Chapters. He was the country's first African American scholarship recruit having grown up in the projects, and although our experiences at Tulane were very different, our perspectives were surprisingly in tune with one another. He went on to explain that he too was one of those creative right brained visual thinkers like myself and that I ought to move to LA and work on this project with him. He stated boldly, "Brian, I don't really think you want to be a doctor." To which I responded, and keep in mind I was still high on Ritalin at the time, "Well maybe, but I feel like I might be able to invent something one day, or elaborate on string theory, maybe develop the physical theory of everything." He was quiet after that response, as I internalized my own laughter, not knowing fully if I was serious with that statement or not. I told him I needed to think about it after talking to him a little while longer.

I called my buddy Rob Pepitone the next day and told him I'm moving to LA in a week and offered him a chance to come along for the ride. Rob had spent the last couple months meditating and growing his own personal garden in his parents' back yard and I knew the kid needed a change. I figured California was more his vibe and he agreed it was time to get out of Holmdel. My silver Audi A4 was so completely saturated with both of our belongings that we literally had no view out the back windshield. The car felt heavy as I backed out a couple feet only to smash into some sort of immovable object only seconds into our trip. This object turned out to be Rob's brother's girlfriend's car and it was at that point, still with 2700 plus miles to California that I knew nothing would go wrong, despite the odds. The only annoying impediment that was bound to materialize itself in one way or another, occurred not more than three feet closer to our destination. I assured Chris' girlfriend that I'd pay for the damages and we were on our way. Goodbye New Jersey, Goodbye Pre-med, goodbye Psychiatrists, goodbye convention. It was time to step into a different realm altogether.

I had printed out a map quest just before grabbing Rob. From: Holmdel, NJ, Destination: Los Angeles California. We tore through North Western NJ crossing the Delaware water gap into Pennsylvania doing one-hundred miles per hour easily heading West on Interstate 80. Rob was a bit anxious at first, as he nibbled on his jarred up figs but the situation soon eased into itself nicely. We made our first stop somewhere West of Cleveland at a Motel 8 in somewhere Ohio. Ohio to me still felt too close, mentally at least, in terms of pushing into my future. Ohio reminded me of Allie and her home outside Cleveland, and Allie was still a touchy subject in my heart, and furthermore we were only two states West of Jersey. We awoke early the next morning skipping breakfast determined to hit the road hard. The yellow of Ohio transitioned into the light green of Indiana by the afternoon. Before we knew it Gary, Indiana was in our rearview mirror as we crossed into Illinois. I gave Allie a call letting her know we were not far outside of Chicago, her current city of residence and she eagerly invited us to stop in and say hello.

From farmland to urban metropolis, Chicago manifested itself within our consciousness first from a distance, where we could see the faded image of buildings tall and densely situated amongst each other like some sort of exclusive high school click standing in an imperfect circular formation. As we came closer the city felt as if it was above us, rather than in front of us. If I hadn't known New York as well as I do, I might have been more impressed by its magnitude, but it was never the less the largest city we were going to pass through until LA. We ended up picking a random street looking to head in the direction of the heart of the city and parked. We were more or less correct and ended up paying $10 to keep our car in a lot downtown. In NYC it would have been triple that.

Allie ended up bailing in accordance to her boyfriend's wishes, but her friend Caroline ended up meeting up with Rob and I and we taxied it over to the artsy district where she was more than hospitable, offering us a place to stay for the night while grabbing dinner with us followed by a rendezvous at one of her neighborhood bars. I wasn't completely upset at Allie but was a bit hurt that she invited us in only to flake out last second. She is ADHD like I am and I understand that we sometimes act impulsively without completely thinking things through. She told me later that she knew I would have started up with her boyfriend. She may have had a point. In any case Caroline and I got drunk together into the early morning. Being a Tulane graduate herself, and a New Orleans Native, we just kept pouring glass upon glass of red and white wine followed by a few beers until we were both blitzed. She began mumbling about how she got a 1530 on her SATS and how all the "Niggers", ruined the city post Katrina. I shot back at her about the Southern racist mentality that reinforces the repression of blacks in the south, and that it was truly deep how she could be so shallow. Her eyes widened as she absorbed the comment and subsequently offered for me to sleep in her bed. We were both blitzed and she was in her thong. Tempting, but I knew it would be a bad idea considering she was a friend of Allie's.

I woke up the next morning to hear Rob and Caroline babbling about something in a far off room, and we hit the road heading west brushing briefly over the boarder of Wisconsin before heading South-West into Iowa, the real garden state. Iowa to me was one of the grandest stretches of road and landscape I have ever seen, with a plush saturated green that was nearly hypnotizing in the peak of sunlight. I felt as if time was non-existent and only temperature and light governed the existence of the rolling farmland that seemed to stretch out into infinity. We stopped at a gas station to fill up and grab some spicy beef jerky and I gave the land around me an intensely focused look through my mind's eye and I felt like I was literally in a geographic vacuum, as if the time space continuum had not fully resolved itself sitting leaning against my car in Iowa. Or maybe it was me who had not resolved me and the vacuum was of the mind, a place of no time, and no space, but only consciousness. For a moment there was no past, and no future, but only the stillness of a psyche that was free to wander.

We loaded back in the car and by evening we had crossed over the Nebraskan border. "Welcome to the Good Life", the sign read. I guess if the good life is in Nebraska then we really had no reason to drive all the way to LA, but something told me to push on. While we had displaced ourselves from the lush green of Iowa, and returned to the universe's regularly scheduled space-time experience, Rob and I were both a bit disappointed at the landscape's return to yellowish brown, as if we were back in Ohio. Fortunately our perception changed as the sun began to dip and we were treated to the most divine sunset, light and colors you could only dream of. The Nebraska sky literally made us feel like we were stoned out of our minds, the only difference being I was driving just fine. It began to rain just as the sun fully disappeared and the aromas of the farm land revealed themselves with true olfactory bliss. Then we looked up at the clearest sky I know for a fact I will ever see. Nebraska *was* the good life, I thought to myself as I began to see signs for Denver popping up, but I knew it was never going to be my life, as good is a relative term, and what's good is not always what's right, as it can never be considered an objective ideal, but merely one's own perception of what pleases them, and these are the types of things that vary from individual to individual. To me Nebraska was good, but certainly not right for me.

Rob began to doze off as we crossed over the Colorado border. We swiped through the city of Denver as I began to wonder where the hell the legendary Rocky Mountains were. The defining and monumental moment of truly reaching the "West" began in my mind at the beginning of our ascent into the Rockies, and before I had time to obsess over the notion, my car was suddenly pointed about 45 degrees closer to the sky as I could feel the magnitude of the enormous bulge beneath my tires. That was it; a pure rush of neurostimulated liberation rushed through my veins and into my head as I knocked the Audi back a gear to handle the ferocious incline. I felt like I had reached the next frontier of my life, from an old boy to a young man. I drove with the sense that I was now in control of my own life, leaving NJ and its expectations behind. The west represented freedom to me, and I wasn't even thinking about Los Angeles, as we still had a lot of road ahead, but I felt as if I could finally look ahead through my own two eyes, without a community of approving or even disapproving eyes looking back at me. I was in control, and life expands with courage, a lesson only learnable through experience.

It was around 1am when we stopped off at some random exit to stock up on energy drinks and other snacks. We subsequently chose to stop at a rest stop nearby and catch some much needed shut eye. Rob and I both reclined our seats as much as possible, which was only about a half an inch for each of us considering the cargo load behind us. Rob fell asleep instantly as I struggled to even close my eyes. I felt a sudden spark of impulsive inspiration to reach Utah by sunrise. I spent the next 5 or so hours tearing through the Rockies. The feeling was like a refined cross between Disney World's Space Mountain and Germany's Audubon. I was weaving speedily, dipping and rising, as the Rocky Mountains became my bitch. As the landscape began to flatten out for a bit, I saw signs indicating that I was closing in on the Utah border. There were random developments and little towns as I continued driving, until suddenly, that which I could only feel, being it had been dark the whole time riding through Colorado, became visible to me in the close distance. It was the next set of mountainous terrain, and the beginning of Utah.

Rob awoke just as we crossed over the border, literally shocked. Picture traveling through Nebraska, the last bit of light we had known at the time, falling asleep, not very far into a dark Colorado, only to awaken in Utah surrounded by the dark red mountainous plateaus representing the next variant of the Rockies. We passed an exit shortly after the border labeled the Trail Through Time, and I almost stopped to check it out until I reminded myself that my journey thus far, and that which remains ahead resonates as my own trail through time. About ten minutes later I pulled to the side of the road, snapped a photo of the sun rising behind us, and switched to the passenger side for some much needed rest. Rob took the wheel as we decided to detour heading into the linear path we had mapped out to check out Arches National Park. We were once again weaving our way within the mountain. We were about 20 minutes into our tangential adventure when I asked Rob to stop the car. We were on a bridge with what I believed to be the Colorado River below us, and I was almost paralyzed by the natural beauty around me. Looking through my panoramic scope, I saw a bridge not too far off in the distance, paralleling the one we were standing on, beyond that and simultaneously behind me, and really all around me were the magnificent iron oxide red cliffs. It was unreal. As my head gyroscoped around once more, I caught a glimpse of a group camping on the small portion of beach like terrain paralleling the river. Their canoes were docked as it was clear that they had not reached their final destination.

It took about another 20 minutes to reach the Park, which turned out to be gigantic, spanning 119 square miles. We drove around from arch to arch, stopping in various spots to go hiking.

Rob was prepared to scale some pretty tough angles with his sneakers. I ended up tossing my sandals to the side to climb barefoot, thereby eliminating the slippage factor almost entirely. My feet tractioned nicely against the dry and somewhat sandy rock as I met Rob atop a solid 40 foot mound. We then moved onward to the edge of a cliff looking over what must have been a thousand foot drop. Toward the edge we looked around to see numerous stacks of rock, most of them about four or five in number placed on top of each other in a descending order by size as the formations rose vertically. I supposed these piles of Rock symbolized some sort of territorial mark of trespass for those who had made it to that point prior to our arrival. Alternatively, it could have been some sort of ancient Native American tribute to the gods. To me they symbolized bravery, and I scanned the ground for quite awhile looking for the piece that would serve as the foundation to my own pile of rocks. I found a few other pieces rather quickly after that, and capped my project off with a somewhat pyramidal top piece and walked away. I subsequently sat down dangling my legs over the cliff as I took in the endless view of valleys and mountains.

When we left Utah, Rob was adamant in regards to the "energy" of the mountains. I agreed with him, as the magnitude of their presence was irresistibly emotive, but something about the obviousness of the statement made me laugh at him. I instantly felt a pain in my heart as I knew I hurt his feelings, but I knew Rob was decades away from being the Buddhist master he thought himself to be at that very moment, as brilliant as he obviously was.. As we carried on through the desert we tore through a piece of Arizona just before hitting Nevada. The landscape really didn't change much from there on, with the Rockies to our right rolling past just as fast as I was driving, albeit in the opposite direction. It was summer time in the hottest geographical section of the United States; the air was thirsty as the desert consumed our imaginations. It had been almost 2000 miles in 2 and a half days and my car deserved a rest, as even camels need water from time to time.

In the far vista of my perception and the foggy haze of the scalding heat, there was a mirage, an oasis perhaps derivative of my wild imagination, thought I wasn't on drugs at the time. No it was for real. Las Vegas materialized like an industrial bubble amongst an infinite plain of steam and light. We headed straight for it and Rob and I split a $60 room about a mile off the main strip. I believe it was the Happy Holiday motel, though it doesn't really matter. We walked toward the casinos, conversating with a homeless man for a good portion of our walk. The entire time he was trying to sell us a rose for our girlfriends, only the rose was missing a petal or two, much like the man himself. We hit the Hard Rock Hotel after a brief taxi ride where Rob and I decided to try our luck with the Casinos. I lost $20 almost instantaneously on the slots and made $80 back in a couple rounds of black jack. I could tell Rob thought gambling was a sin of some sort, according to his ever changing moral philosophy of the moment, and was rooting against me secretly so that I may learn my lesson. I'd say I've learned enough lessons in my day and that some things were just never going to change, for instance, my intrigue with anything involving risk and the supposed unconquerable. Not to say that black jack qualifies as unconquerable, but the speed at which we reached Vegas leaving from Jersey not so many afternoon's ago I'd reckon would be tough for anyone to beat.

With the flashing lights and the constant temptations I felt the impulsive ADHD chaos streaming through my veins once again, perhaps over stimulated, and that was before I began drinking at the Steele Pulse concert outside by the pool. I remember downing a few Red Bull Vodkas to try and keep pace, being that I had been up since two mornings prior, having driven all night through Colorado and spending the day hiking in Utah. The who and the where of what I am was streaming back and forth in an almost foreign circular momentum. We ended up crashing until about 11:00am the next day, prepared mentally for the last leg of our trip cross country. LA was theoretically about 5 hours away. The landscape was similar to the way it had been since Arizona though I could feel we were getting close. When we hit the California Inspection at the border, I felt a surge of excitement and Euphoria. The female officer asked us quickly if we were harboring any illegal produce, which looking back was a pretty hilarious question to ask at any border, be it Nevada to California, or South Korea to North Korea. No! We were not harboring any illegal "produce" or even weapons of mass destruction…just a little bit of LSD. We carried on and intentionally passed the exit for Hollywood so that I10 would dwindle down to past exit one and we had no choice but to introduce our presence to the Pacific Ocean, the monument of the end of our trip. Dark blue and marvelous gleaming in the sunlight, I snapped a photograph. We had arrived.

Chapter 12: Hollywood

Rob and I had just torn through the country with a feel for

the landscape that one can only obtain from driving state by state,

mental state by mental state. We were exhausted as we found the

studio I had impulsively chosen without giving much thought as to

its exact geographical whereabouts. It was Hollywood, that was

really all that mattered, and my mind felt like it had just gone

through some sort of time warp to get there. Not far north of us

were the hiking trails of Runyon Canyon, and all around us were

some very interesting characters. My perception of self at that point

was in flux having traveled so far to reach a destination I knew

nothing about, except that having gone to college in New Orleans,

lived in Shanghai for a period of time, and New York City after

that, perhaps it was wanderlust that kept me going. I had resolved

myself, however, that I get a good feel for the city, and even if I

were to move out of Hollywood, I would stay in California, most

likely closer to the beach in Santa Monica now that I think about it.

In Hollywood the phonies were as numerous as they were easily identifiable, but there really was something to the genuine characters found in the area. Of all the stereotypes surrounding Hollywood, for instance "everything is phony", "nothing is real", or my favorite, "the land of the crazy people", were simultaneously true and ultimately false. If the world is just an image within my mind, as it has been scientifically proven that there is no absolute proof of a world outside of your own head, then what is reality to begin with? If that is such a crazy notion; another relative term, then perhaps I am a little crazy. Out here in Hollywood the "crazy" people, for those who really understand the situation, are considered artists, writers, actors, and so forth. They are human, many of them just trying to get by on their talent within one of the most competitive industries in the world, the entertainment business. I for one was not caught up in the potential success of this new project of mine, as I was still unsure whether I cared about success as society would view it, and was pretty much convinced at the time that 2700 miles away from home, the last thing I was going to do is let this idea of accumulating wealth and the mentality that coincides with it follow me after working so hard and fast to get the hell out of the Northeast.

Really it was a nice situation for all of us. My parents were able to bask in the fact that their son was out in LA working with Mr. Harold Sylvester, Emmy award winner, and I was just happy to once again discover and wander through new realms in Los Angeles, CA, and yes of course I was aware that there was business to take care of. I called Harold up a few days after I arrived and we made plans for me to travel up to North Hollywood, which is in the valley, not too far from where I was living. I was excited to meet Harold, but not the least bit intimidated. I was just thrilled that someone of such talent had recognized my abilities, and furthermore, from our conversation a couple weeks ago, I knew we were like minded. I remember I had made it to his house giving myself plenty of time taking into consideration I had no idea where I was without the directions I had copied from map quest, and aside from that the traffic in LA is as reflectively insane and chaotic as the people inhabiting the city itself.

When I pulled into Harold's neighborhood it felt like any other somewhat suburban neighborhood with modest houses, all of them rather similar lining the sidewalk spaced out efficiently, except for one, which I knew without looking was Harold's house, partially fortified behind two beautiful fences made entirely of green shrubbery with a white wooden outline, which served to block out the view of most of the house. There was no gate per se, as the driveway was shaped like a "U", allowing people and automobiles to enter and exit freely, but the high fence nevertheless stood for prominence, as if to say, there better be a good reason to pass through...Luckily I had my ticket. I parked on the curb out of respect as I normally do when I visit anyone and walked over the grass, passing through the looped driveway rather than around it. I was a bit lost at first, as I wasn't sure if I was to enter through the front door of his house. I gave him a call to let him know I had arrived and he told me to come to his office, which stood adjacent to the house, looking like a smaller version of the house itself. The whole exterior in accordance with my vision reminded me of the American Dream. He had a nicely sized piece of land (not cheap in

S. California), with a rather large white wooden paneled house with, in accordance to what I remembered, green window panes.

I was about thirty feet from his office down the straightened portion of his driveway which extended like a tangent off a parabola when he came out to greet me. Neither of us said a word to each other between the drama of my approach, as I recall seeing him evaluate me with a hard glance all the while I was wondering if he thought me to be a Nazi, with my newly shaved head and side burns. Really I had been shaving my head on and off since eighth grade, not to get caught in the tangent I was currently walking, but he was Black and he knew I was Jewish, so most likely he did not see me as a Nazi. There was no emotion attached to these thoughts racing through my mind, but merely a cerebral adventure of sorts to kill the time before I'd finally shake his hand. I extended my hand out to greet him and asked him in a cool, manner, "Hey, man how ya doing?" He responded in what was probably an even cooler manner, "Heyy Brian, getting old" We subsequently went inside and sat down on the couch where I noticed a silver plate with a partially smoked cigar laying on top as if to radiate cool success. We sat down on the couch as we instantaneously began to talk about how both of us had struggled with society's conception of our own identities, and I went on to explain how I was not an anti-Semite by any means, and had literally beat the shit out of individuals on occasion that ever dared call myself or any of my friends a kyke. My friend Blake could certainly attest to that, as I think back to a specific altercation in a pizza joint in New York's West Village.

It was clear to me that we both cared deeply for the people we supposedly belonged to, though at his point in life he was probably more comfortable with his own feelings on the subject then I was. Harold struck me as a proud Black man, and a free man with many achievements to back it up, including being the first Black NCAA Division 1 scholarship athlete for Basketball, on top of his success as an actor in the incredibly competitive entertainment business, including roles in "Officer and A Gentleman", and Griff on "Married with Children." As a writer he had been given high praise for the made for TV movie, "Passing Glory". He wrote a few episodes for "NYPD Blue" and had even won an Emmy for his role as producer of the documentary "On Hallowed Ground."

When we sat down at his desk his son Harold joined us as we began to look at the characters I had drawn up for the pilot we were about to begin working on. In between work he was telling me about his younger radical days when he used to attend Black Panther rallies and get tear gassed from time to time. He was trying to explain, as he told me simply, "I was a radical just like you are." He fought for civil rights the way I would have fought in his position, not with peaceful integration into a system that was clearly oppressive and lacked true acknowledgement of the needs of the black people in those days, but with the threat of radical change by any means necessary. I don't know the exact details of what went down in those days, though I doubt he ever laid a hand on anybody, unless somebody came at him the wrong way. I see the public school system in the same manner. Just because the majority of kids in school fit within a certain mold does not mean that they have the right to deny the many gifted kids falling through the cracks. This very idea equates to the denial of opportunity. From a Black man's perspective I would have fought with passion during the civil rights movement because when there is oppression, there is tyranny, and submissive obedience will never get the job done in such a situation. Not in society and not in the class room.

Harold, in his late fifties, the man sitting in front of me as I try and process all that he was trying to tell me about himself, was a true hero in my eyes, and I was honored to be in his presence. Despite all the passion I knew he possessed, he is one of the coolest and laid back individuals I had ever met. No Hollywood attitude or sense of entitlement, just mutual respect. I left that day feeling my whole world had shifted gears. Harold Sylvester, no matter when our project comes to fruition, did me a great favor. If not for him I would have still been abusing nasty ADD drugs in a frustrating attempt at doing something considered along the lines of being a nice Jewish boy. Really every attempt I had made to be what I perceived as a nice Jewish boy had been drug induced. Harold showed me that freedom is possible, and to him I am very grateful. Though I am still on my own quest to find within me what he eventually found within himself.

I came to learn that the entertainment business really is nothing like any other business, especially Wall Street, where everything happens with intense speed and direct linear responses. Hollywood I soon realized was not the type of business one should ever attach expectations to in terms of a timetable. Just as my intuitive sense of time is that it is a man made invention for the sake of scheduling ourselves, I think Hollywood, or LA for that matter may be the only place on earth that actually abides by the notion of timelessness. The sun will shine without any real sense of seasons meanwhile everyone is just trying to get their project noticed. Even Harold, an established artist with success and a little bit of fame could not just push a button to get a show on TV.

On coincidence, just as I moved to Hollywood, the writer's strike had just come to fruition which proved to be an extremely frustrating time for me as Harold and I couldn't even progress with our project, let alone present it. I took to smoking a lot of wonderfully potent pot and drinking as I've always done. The pot in

LA was incredible, and much of it was straight out of Uncle Sam's laboratory, aka medicinal marijuana, the legal type only found in California. I had liquidated my 401K which was pretty stacked after a year at Morgan Stanley. All my money was in Emerging Markets, and ended up providing me with about 6 months of rent without having to get a job. Looking back it was the wrong way to go about things because I have been known to be quite self destructive when the activities of the day, everyday, revolved around Hindu Kush (weed) and Beer of all varieties. Socially I was my usual self, scattered among various groups including the potheads living above me, a pretty girl named Megan down the hall, and a few on and off girl friends here and there. I was basically procrastinating until I needed to get a job, typical of someone with ADHD, but considering the amount of money I was spending on alcohol; clearly there was more going on.

I was considerably depressed having moved out to California knowing nobody. The furniture in my studio consisted of a futon mattress and the bongo left behind by Rob when he flew back to Jersey. I was considerably alone, feeling much like my days in NY where I was enclosed in depression and isolated. I would take a lot of walks and work on the project here and there, but everything was moving so slowly and I felt empty living and spaced out under the eternal sunshine of Los Angeles. I began to hike Runyon Canyon between occasionally socializing with people I knew I could never really let in as friends, and drinking myself silly. It was probably the one healthy endeavor I had insisted upon. I would hike up what is probably about a good mile and a half in altitude with terrain that was tiered similarly to the Great Wall of China, though of course lacking the brick by brick composure of the Great Wall. I began to lose a lot of weight after committing myself to three times a week hiking up and then trekking down the canyon. It was beautiful at the top on a clear day. Looking west you could see the Santa Monica Mountains stretching out into the Pacific Ocean, straight ahead was Hollywood and looking east you could see Downtown LA, and at the very top point of the mountain, you are literally above it all, as if LA is some sort of foreign object down below.

As I looked down, my depression grew deeper as I was still fairly new in the city and the project was stalled indefinitely due to the writer's strike. I was wondering why I still wasn't happy. Perhaps it was because even with all the distance between myself and the money chasing mentality I thought I had to be a part of to make the family proud, I was still logically in the same situation. I was fully expected to make it huge in Hollywood, an industry worth Billions. I resolved myself that I would not return to the Northeast, not even for a visit, before I made it big. At least that was one side of my story in CA. From another perspective I began to see LA as a place for drifters, and I felt like a drifter at heart myself. I loved just chilling out on a park bench at the top of Runyon Canyon, or near the sand in Venice beach. My friend Ashley told me about a band of counterculture rebel rich kids in Venice who chose to disown all the privilege and expectations of the scripted life being born into a wealthy family and literally chose to be homeless on the street under the warmth of the Venice sun.

I had already known what it was like to be homeless, at least for a day in China, in about 6 degree weather, and I found it to be one of the most awakening and life affirming days of my life. Maybe I should be homeless for a while with the hippies at Venice beach. Obviously homelessness is not all that it's cracked up to be, but I figured maybe I wanted to really suffer and see what it was like to sink to the bottom. This was right around the time my friend Justin flew in to visit. I picked him up at the airport and put the homeless idea on hold for a bit as I showed him the various sights of Hollywood and the surrounding LA area. I even agreed to meet some of his friends for Shabbat dinner, just to see how I would react after all these years. We ended up meeting a few of his buddies at some sort of Hebrew school where all these orthodox Jews were chanting one of my least favorite languages. I met the Rabbi in charge of rounding up the young LA Jews in the community and he immediately attempted to hand me a yamaka, to which I declined. The others kind of gave me a look but Justin knew what to expect. I told the Rabbi, "I do not want to disrespect you, and if that is the case then I will leave". He gave me an evaluating glance and told me no, "I would not be disrespecting him"

We sat down for about twenty minutes as they recited prayers out of the Torah as I remained silent as I scanned the room, half day dreaming, half aware of the 5 different Rabbis that approached the table in consecutive order within about 2 minute increments, placing yamaka after yamaka on my table. With each yamaka, the Rabbi I was with took them and placed them under his prayer book until the book itself had an almost buoyant quality to it as it was now lopsided and fluffed up sitting above 5 crumpled up Jew hats. After the prayer session we went back to his house where his wife had cooked up a true feast at the dinner table. In between bites I remained silent as the rest of the table recited prayers, though there was one thing different about this Shabbat dinner that was unlike the last Shabbat dinner I had attended 10 years ago: We were all taking shots of Jack Daniels in between prayers, which certainly helped to ease my anxiety considering the context of my whereabouts and staying with my principles. As the night went on, I had watched as the others continued to recite prayers here and there as we had all moved on to single malt scotch.

Perhaps a little Jack was exactly what I needed to withstand Hebrew school back in the day, which is more or less what I had pronounced to the Rabbi as the dinner carried on. I began to debate him about how people were killing each other over religion and that if we could all abide by a code of solid ethics unattached to some sort of supernatural deity attached to it, we would no longer have the need to kill in the name of this or that "G-d". Jesus for instance preached peace and honor; meanwhile how many millions upon millions of people have died, really murdered in his name, all the while representing the polar opposite of everything Jesus stood for? Religion, as I saw it was truly the anti-Christ, the root of all evil alongside greed, which often times it is difficult to distinguish between the two. We went back and forth for awhile, all the while taking shots of Whisky and Scotch to end the night. I left very grateful for what turned out to be an interesting and most delicious evening. I had nothing but respect for the Rabbi as he tried to invite me back for next Shabbat dinner. I told him he can count on me in another 10 years from the very date…We compromised on 5.

Later that week, my new friend Dave introduced me to a girl running trips to Israel. Basically every Jewish young adult under the age of 26 can sign up for a free ride under a program called Birth Right Israel. I told her I was the kid that always got suspended in Hebrew school for lashing out and that I certainly doubted I would enjoy myself among some sort of religious tour through the "home land". She smiled and told me, "Yeah, I remember the kids like you", she paused, "They were always the most sensitive one's." I suppose she was right. Despite the tough guy attitude I carried and the whole idea that nothing affects me and everyone is stupid, I really am a very sensitive kid. It's just that I've learned to block out my emotions, and in doing that, my sensitivity toward the world has often translated into thunderous outbursts of discontent and anger… She was right, but I still wasn't signing up.

Chapter 13: Rehab

The drinking worsened with time to the point where half my studio apartment gleamed with the refracted light of sunshine divided through the mound of empty bottles piled idly in the kitchen and hallway. The life of a young man whose life revolves around bottles of Trappist monk brewed Chimay and benzodiazepines to keep him down was probably going to bottom out sometime soon, especially with the assistance of the crystal meth rocks given to him by his latest wacko psychiatrist in his Hollywood apartment overlooking Santa Monica Blvd. Among the white blaze of crystal meth looping through his synapses, morphed a shining moment of clarity. He made a phone call...

"Dad: I'm high on meth, and constantly wasted, and have been for the last 9 months or so. I should probably go to rehab."

Pause:

"Ok Bri, your plane leaves tomorrow. We love you."

I went back to the crystallized rock that was adderall to the nth degree and inhaled repeatedly throughout the remainder of the night. The psychiatrist decided to warn me that crystal meth is an addictive substance, as if he had just written me a script for a take home regimen, and needed to comply with proper medicinal guidelines associated with the distribution of a controlled substance. I smiled deviously in his face as I turned on his stove and almost instantaneously transformed his entire stash of crystalline-methamphetamine into a dense cloud of hazardous smoke, and subsequently took the cloud deep into my lungs, before I blew out with hateful satisfaction.

"See ya, Doc" I explained in a speedy trance. "Sure he explained in a somewhat bewildered manner, I'll see you around, I'm sure."

"Nope, you won't.... I'm heading to rehab, enjoy the rest of your time in hell"

And, say goodbye to Hollywood...

I'm in Arizona inside the mountainous terrain of outer

Tucson. There are coyotes howling in the background, as the new

backdrop of the latest update of my reality provides me with a

feeling of safety from myself. They drug test me and find all the

meth in my system, even though I had already disclosed to them

every drug I had taken in the past few months, consisting of Meth

(which I had only done twice), and some cocaine, which I had done

more than twice, but never heroine, as much as I would have liked

to have tried it, rehab would have to be a onetime thing, and I

would therefore never have the opportunity to do heroine.

I walked around during my first day with needle pricks lodged into

my socks and the skin on my shins drawing blood droplets as a

result of walking into a few cactus plants during the preliminary

discoveries of my new home. There was a green band around my wrist indicative of the fact that I was now a voluntary patient in a drug and alcohol rehabilitation facility. I looked around at the people who were thought to be in the same position as me and I couldn't relate to them. These people had problems. I was just passing time. Living like I was living was a choice, I didn't need to drink, and didn't even crave it when I wasn't. I wasn't weak like these people, and these people would never be my friends. We were nothing alike.

I showed up to my fist counseling session seeming to think that it was a classroom of sorts. Lizzy, the social worker assigned to me, and a few others, was a sweet old British lady whom I took an instant liking to. She had me introduce myself to the group, consisting of two girls from Houston, one of them a pretty blond suck up investment banking type who just finished up work on her MBA and was on extended leave from Merrill Lynch. She had her redeeming qualities, but her clear lack of core self identity left her with a personality that you could peel off willingly, as with an onion where the layers disintegrate with a simple cut, and you are left with a foul stench and stinging eyes.

The other girl from Houston was more interesting. She was overweight and unattractive, with an eating disorder and an alcohol problem. She was later determined to suffer from Anti-Social Personality disorder, which is the latest euphemistic declaration of what was once referred to as being a sociopath. I'd say her clear disregard for the feelings of others came off much more genuine than the overdone superficial attempts that Paige would put forth, like a Girl Scout whose merit badges were traded in for a six figure income as an adult, a wardrobe exclusively designed by J-Crew and Polo, a two bedroom condo, "away from the dredges of society", (as she would put it), and bulimia.

I'd say I was annoyed by almost everything about Paige, and I struggled with great difficulty not to lose my composure completely when I found out eight months later that she broke her neck and died after falling down her stairs in her condo wasted on mediocre wine and a half bottle of Ambien. Apparently she hated herself beyond anyone else's opinion of her. This was a sad girl and I should have been nicer to her. I don't know why I wasn't. The initial days were difficult for me as I was having a tough time complying with all the rules at Sierra Tucson. I was uncooperative during the large meetings where everyone would get together and listen to the various updates and newsworthy events prefacing the upcoming week of activities and therapy sessions. These were the same meetings where we would end in a gigantic circle and beg of G-d to, "help us to accept the things that we cannot change". I for one would not step in the circle, and I was certainly not going to partake in a mass chanting like members of a religious cult would orchestrate. Paige later remarked that it made her sad when I didn't join the circle.

I didn't want to make her sad.

I told my Jewish friend Sam about my hesitation to join the circle since I wasn't sure about G-d to begin with. He tapped me forcibly over the head with the open palm of a book as if to suggest that there is something higher than my own existence. I guess I always supposed their might be, but it never actually hit me like that. I gave it some deep thought, however. Apparently, as it was explained by one of the spiritual guides at rehab, the idea of G-d, in terms of reaching out toward a higher power, was not specific to any one finite entity, but rather, the importance of the connection was that there was some notion at all, no matter how abstract of a conception. I came to realize that my unwillingness to share things about myself, and let others in was affecting the group at large. The energy of my nonparticipation was contagious, and my reluctant attitude was impeding the progress of others.

I wouldn't call this G-d, per say, but I did begin to see that I was part of something larger, and if I could let people in just a little bit, I would thereby stand in acknowledgement that I wasn't being utterly selfish after witnessing the reciprocal effects on other people derivative of a more positive attitude on my part. It wasn't just about me... I began to look around and discovered a sense of connectedness with the people around me that I had never felt before. I came to realize the unconscious power and support that community is able to provide, and my guard dropped down a little so that I could soak in this spherical feeling of inertial entanglement.

Slowly these people became my friends, and I felt myself transforming through the layers of my sadness and regret as they were working hard to deal with their own demons. The Arizona sun beamed light into my cracked mind and my mind reflected back

with tenacious transference. I was becoming symbiotic with nature

again, as my heroin addict friend Dave and I would sneak off

campus to rummage through deserted trails in the mountains,

navigating carefully through thickets of cacti and prickly brush. We

would skip rocks into the dense terrain to try to lure animals out of

hiding, though it proved to be unsuccessful. Dave was another

good friend that I can only assume is still alive, though I did hear he

overdosed sometime later on in LA, only to be sentenced back to

some sort of stricter institution. I'm not sure if they let him back to

University of Pennsylvania.

Group therapy sessions became less of a fight as a few weeks

passed. I would speak about my days in Hebrew school and how it

underscored some of the issues I would have with my own self

identity later. Lizzy described my days in Hebrew School as a source

of "trauma" in my life. Rehabilitation specialists are big on

detecting, "*TRAUMA*". I 'd say the majority of the trauma

involved with my reign at Temple Shalom was largely absorbed by

the poor instructors who were assigned to the likes of me, but so be

it ...I came to realize, through the help of the spoken word and a series of sessions, that it was up to me to differentiate between the potential for the love and support that originates out of Judaism and the warmth inherent inside the spirit of the people, from the terrible time I had with the forced indoctrination of , as I saw it, illegitimate knowledge and the brainwashing of impressionable minds (not mine). I came to realize that intellectual curiosity, and the unwillingness to take accepted notions of anything at face value, even if it be the belief system of your "own people", is a very Jewish thing indeed. Some of the greatest thinkers throughout the ages were of Jewish decent, and many were non-practicing or non-religious.

My battle was clearly with myself. I didn't need to drink because I wasn't a millionaire yet, and I don't need to waste myself in oblivion if I never become one. There are just as many Jewish individuals that live modest lives working for charities or non-profit organizations as there are flashy litigators and financiers. Nobody remembers or even cares how much Jews like Einstein or Freud had left in their estate when they died. There are larger issues at hand; like self fulfillment. My battle with the Jewish people has always been a battle with myself, as most things seen as unlikable about others tends to originate from the war inside themselves. I left rehab with a sense that at 24 years old it was not too late to start over and become a better person.

I finally end up back in New York--first Brooklyn, and finally Manhattan--after deciding to choose life rather than impending death, albeit it is still life in my own way. The chaos has toned down as I have done the best I can to plant new seeds and reach out to some of my old roots, roots that I thought I had been torn from long ago, but to my pleasant surprise, have remained and exist with the potential to strengthen and evolve. With the addition of some new post-rehab friends, and the reconnection with friends of old, there is a new found feeling of respect and acceptance of myself, and hence the world I inhabit. I no longer wish to hide. I am what I am, even if I seem to be in outer space often times, this is certainly better than laying underground. It's ok if you see me as different, because I see you as different, and in a way, that makes us the same, and above all I have found purpose. I have made a rough peace not just with the 13 tribes of Israel but all the tribes of the world. Despite my differences and difficulties, I am, just as everyone like me, a human being, dear reader. I am you.

Maybe I can even be a good boy? A good Jewish boy???...

Don't push it.

Epilogue:

What is happening here is that when there is assumption that everyone is inside the box and thinking outside of it is like taking a break from a regularly scheduled activity, you teach to the exclusion of those who live their life, OUTSIDE THE BOX. For me, thinking inside the box is sometimes just as hard as it is for someone else to think outside of it. For one, I have trouble thinking about one specific idea without attempting to generalize and connect this idea as a concept with a seemingly altogether different domain of knowledge. Sometimes in the midst of my attempt to make connections, I will stumble upon an all together different ideas, far away from where I started, though still relevant in its own way.

John Locke was a famous British philosopher of the seventeenth century who wrote extensively on the theory of knowledge. To summarize, his theory revolves around the "Tabula Rasa", or blank slate, and that knowledge is obtained as we build upon this blank slate like the construction of a building, the framework for which is obtained through ideas laid down as concepts. In other words, the purpose of knowledge is to build an intricate framework of concepts that are able to mold together and universally connect as we as humans come into more and more contact with seemingly isolated ideas. We are constantly building upon what we already know in order to gain a more complex, and holistic body of knowledge and understanding of the world we live in. Somewhere along the line the educational system has lost track of this understanding and instead of willing its students toward a global perspective of knowledge and thought, we have instead began to compartmentalize facts and ideas so that they remain merely isolated colonies of thought without any sort of unifying framework.

Perhaps the reason for this is that society is more concerned with training our minds to think in isolated chunks of the whole because one day, for the sake of the economy, we will have to choose a specialization of some sort for our occupations. Our minds are becoming more and more suited for the tiny little cubes most workers will call their desks representing a small part of a rather large institutional whole, like isolated atoms of thought orbiting with a loose connectivity to the larger molecule, easily swayed by the next attractive charge, and ultimately lost in a web of disassociation. For the sake of the economy I do not have a problem with an educational system that wishes to ensure the livelihood of tomorrow but we are suppressing the type of thinking that will ultimately lead to innovation rather than being well schooled in the types of things we have already figured out. There are leaders and there are followers, and in many cases, one must be a follower in order to become a leader, but if we continue to educate students like sheep in a herd through repetition of solutions to problems already solved, than we will be a nation representative of an antiquated solution to an antiquated problem.

If on the other hand we can encourage the type of creative thinking not representative of any problem in particular, but rather, representative of the type of thought process involved in universal concepts and creative solutions, we can rid ourselves of the shackles of intellectual underachievement as a society and branch out toward a renewed global presence and respect among the powerhouses of the East. I am not saying that we should by any means stop teaching the same solutions to the same problems entirely, as these solutions represent the bedrock of intellectual and academic advancement in history, what I am saying is we ought to focus more on the thought process behind the intellectual leaders that lead us to these solutions in the first place in order to gain a better understanding of where true academic leadership derives itself from.

On a personal note, things are looking good for me and the future looks bright. I have resolved most of the issues that have been bothering me from the past and writing this manuscript has proved to be quite cathartic in its own right. I feel blessed that I am able to finally express myself through this medium, as there has been so much building up inside me for so long, I fret that without such an outlet, the pressure inside would burst in a less productive and far more destructive manner, as it has too many times in the past. My ego was shot for a long time after high school and I have experienced significant social and emotional withdrawal, a very unhealthy duo of complicated human responses. Looking back, as sequentially as I can manage, I believe I have found the root of the majority of my problems, though to have come this far, there is one thing I am fortunate to know I will never lose, as it has been already been put to the test, and that is my undying faith in myself.

I want to call for freedom. Not to be confused with anarchy, but a matter of liberation so to speak. I am calling for liberation from psychiatric diagnoses that do more harm than good. I am especially calling for the immediate halt in the over prescribing of dangerous personality altering, soul diluting drugs. What people need to realize is that there is no absolute truth, only schools of thought, and when the masses of society lean toward one direction, so too does their frame of mind, not realizing that they are blindly accepting a system of thought that is not necessarily correct, but merely agreed upon by enough people that it is accepted as truth. I want to put a stop to all of this. I want the school system to wake up and realize that there is a new breed of children emerging in epidemic proportions, call them ADHD, what have you, they are out of the box thinkers, many of them gifted in their own right. Whatever it is, when there is oppression of the few, for the sake of the betterment of the masses, expect a thunderous rebellion from those strong enough to recognize and act upon the need for change.

In Hebrew school I was a trouble maker while raising potent philosophical questions that the teachers were not prepared to answer from a young child. I should have behaved right, taken my ADD meds and sat quietly and accepted the status quo? Later on in my life, especially in college I relied heavily on drugs and alcohol to avoid the true introspection necessary to deal with a turbulent past. All the sudden I end up doing a year with Morgan Stanley before my psyche literally exploded with passion and new ideas, ideas that I have been lucky enough to channel into words. My call for mental nationalism is this: Liberate your mind from antiquated systems of thought and will your own meaning upon the world, and do it with passion. Just as countries and states have borders, nationalistic borders that is, so too should the individual. A free thinker wages war on oppressive systems and threats just as a state or country would. If you don't harm me, I won't harm you. I say live and let live, but if you do start telling me how to think, or come at me violently, I will give back to you threefold. This is what I call progress.

I refuse to be depressed having lived a life thus far because Judaism dictates a particular mold of thought and action out of their congregation. If I don't want to recite Hebrew, then I won't. If I choose to give the idea of G-d more thought as I grow and live through new experiences, rather than having the idea shoved down my throat like when I was young, I will. If you choose to debate with me, you will probably lose, though I am surely open to new ideas. If a Rabbi comes to my house and tries to guilt trip me into "honoring" him by attending one of his services, I will tell him no, I don't mean any disrespect, but I cannot do that. I am free to decide, and so too should the rest of this world.

As far as Israel goes, my call for mental nationalism, being the relative term that it is, I don't for one second deny their right to fight for what they see as their land, not because I am Jewish, but because nations and countries have always had to fight for what they perceive as their own. Is it fair to call the Pilgrims illegal aliens when they first arrived upon an already inhabited Native American land called America? Now think about the Mexicans. That is certainly up for debate. The history text books in school would surely not teach it in such a way, as history is written by the victors, but we have to look at things outside of our own perspectives, because that is the only place we will ever find the shades of gray where truth resides. If I am Israel personified, and a bunch of hoodlums with masks and machine guns try and jump me where I stand, proclaiming that where I stand is really where they are meant to stand, then I am going to shove a tank up their asses and shred them to bits, but I'll give them credit for trying. If I am in school and the teacher is trying to indoctrinate me with an idea or thought that I am opposed to, then I am going to state my rebuttal, and he or she has every right to state her own, and we can go back and forth until one of us is right, or we agree to disagree, but as far as authority is concerned, we need to realize that it is a very relative concept, and in reality, that which we know of it, we have to realize that authority is only as potent and real as we actively subject ourselves to it. This is something that I realized at a very early age.

If someone calls you ADD, perhaps someone with "Authority" representing a pseudo science such as psychology or psychiatry, you have every right to say ok, maybe this is a positive thing, and this person can help me out with life and the tribulations surrounding it, but if you care to rise above societies labels and declare yourself to be simply an individual, you have every right to do so. Do I have ADHD? Well that's what doctors have said since I was six. I certainly do not pay attention to much of what is being said to me, and yes I do seem to be far off into my own world at times, so call it what you will, that is your choice, but this is mine: I am what I am. I do not feel the need to pay homage to these arbitrary labels just because I am a unique individual.

I challenge every parent that reads this today, who is dealing with a younger version of a kid similar to me, to take a good look at exactly what you are dealing with. If he or she is sitting in a classroom, day dreaming or disrupting because their mind is not wired like the rest of the class, the last thing you should do is force them to conform. I'd say, if anything, do your best to create an environment that better suits a soaring imagination and a lack of attention toward what the other children are sitting nicely at their desks for. If you work with your kid, they will work with you, if not, these independent minds will find a way to express themselves in a very different, and much more destructive manner. I used to hurl bricks through the windows of unfinished construction sites to get my anger out. In college I boozed and did drugs while purposefully choosing to read books outside of the curriculum. Sure didn't help my GPA, but there was no question I was getting smart. Perhaps I was rebelling, more than likely I was just following my interests. I read Mein Kempf, an autobiographical book written by Hitler just to get inside the head of my enemy. I wondered how a struggling artist like the goofy looking bastard named Adolf could possibly transform a nation into a political tyranny through the illogical rants in his book and through his speeches, and there is really only one answer: Because people let him.

We need to start thinking for ourselves, and liberate our minds. Trust me I am by no means a hippy even if I sound like one at times, (not that there is anything wrong with that), just that for me, weed makes me lazy and I need a job to support myself and to stay of out trouble. I have realized that thought without action is stagnant, and although some may label me as radical, they are missing the point entirely. We need to abolish these notions of categorization in the first place. I am an apolitical person calling for mental nationalism. Live and let live, protect your mental borders, and be careful when crossing the mental borders of others, especially mine if you mean to inflict your belief system, through tyranny, into my domain. I will end where I began, as if to say, an individual's ability, or disability is relative to mental environmental factors. If I'm thinking in pictures about Jupiter's gravitational orbit around the sun, and you are trying to tell me how great it was that Abraham was going to slay his son Isaac on top of a mountain, then we are not communicating, and I am going to let you know. With proper communication we can have peace, from student to teacher, from blue state to red state, from the first world to the third world, and back around again to the fundamental atoms of thought that represent the fabric of my consciousness.

End.

Made in the USA
Lexington, KY
25 August 2010